DON'T DIE
WITH
YOUR MUSIC
STILL IN YOU

Inspirational Thoughts
Making the Shift (6-CD set)
Making Your Thoughts Work for You (with Byron Katie)
Meditations for Manifesting
101 Ways to Transform Your Life (audio book)
The Power of Intention (abridged 4-CD set)
A Promise Is a Promise (audio book)
Secrets of Manifesting
The Secrets of the Power of Intention (6-CD set)
10 Secrets for Success and Inner Peace
There Is a Spiritual Solution to Every Problem
The Wayne Dyer Audio Collection/CD Collection
Wishes Fulfilled (unabridged audio book)

DVDs

Change Your Thoughts—Change Your Life
Excuses Begone!
Experiencing the Miraculous
I Can See Clearly Now
The Importance of Being Extraordinary (with Eckhart Tolle)
Inspiration
My Greatest Teacher (a film with bonus material featuring Wayne)
Modern Wisdom from the Ancient World
The Power of Intention
The Shift, the movie (available as a 1-DVD program and an expanded 2-DVD set)
10 Secrets for Success and Inner Peace
There's a Spiritual Solution to Every Problem
Wishes Fulfilled

MISCELLANEOUS

Change Your Thoughts—Change Your Life Perpetual Flip Calendar
Everyday Wisdom Perpetual Flip Calendar
Inner Peace Cards
Inspiration Perpetual Flip Calendar
The Power of Intention Cards
The Power of Intention Perpetual Flip Calendar
The Shift Box Set (includes *The Shift* DVD and *The Shift* tradepaper book)
10 Secrets for Success and Inner Peace Cards
10 Secrets for Success and Inner Peace gift products:
Notecards, Candle, and *Journal*

All of the above are available at your local bookstore, or may be ordered by visiting: Hay House USA: www.hayhouse.com; Hay House Australia: www .hayhouse.com.au; Hay House UK: www.hayhouse.co.uk; Hay House South Africa: www.hayhouse.co.za; Hay House India: www.hayhouse.co.in

DON'T DIE
WITH
YOUR MUSIC
STILL IN YOU

My Experience Growing Up
with Spiritual Parents

Serena J. Dyer
and
Dr. Wayne W. Dyer

HAY HOUSE, INC.
Carlsbad, California • New York City
London • Sydney • Johannesburg
Vancouver • Hong Kong • New Delhi

Published and distributed in the United States by: Hay House, Inc.: www .hayhouse.com® • *Published and distributed in Australia by:* Hay House Australia Pty. Ltd.: www.hayhouse.com.au • *Published and distributed in the United Kingdom by:* Hay House UK, Ltd.: www.hayhouse.co.uk • *Published and distributed in the Republic of South Africa by:* Hay House SA (Pty), Ltd.: www.hayhouse.co.za • *Distributed in Canada by:* Raincoast Books: www.raincoast.com • *Published in India by:* Hay House Publishers India: www.hayhouse.co.in

Cover design: Amy Rose Grigoriou   *Interior design:* Tricia Breidenthal

The quote from Elisabeth Kübler-Ross on page 50 has been reprinted by permission of the EKR Family Limited Partnership.

Library of Congress Cataloging-in-Publication Data

Dyer, Serena (Serena J.)
  Don't die with your music still in you : my experience growing up with spiritual parents / Serena Dyer and Wayne Dyer. -- 1st edition.
    pages cm
  ISBN 978-1-4019-3627-3 (tradepaper : alk. paper) 1. Dyer, Serena (Serena J.) 2. Spiritual biography. 3. Spiritual life. 4. Life. 5. Conduct of life. 6. Dyer, Wayne W. I. Title.
  BL73.D94A3 2014
  204'.4--dc23

                                2014007801

ISBN: 978-1-4019-3627-3

17 16 15 14   4 3 2 1
1st edition, June 2014

Printed in the United States of America

For my parents

As Rumi once wrote, "You were born with wings,
why prefer to crawl through life?" I thank you, with
every part of my being, for demonstrating this for me.
Everything I am is because of your love for me.
Thank you, thank you, thank you.

CONTENTS

INTRODUCTION
FROM SERENA

Some years ago my father wrote a book called *10 Secrets for Success and Inner Peace,* in which he outlined the ten secrets he hoped his children would live by. Since I am one of his children, and have been raised on these secrets, I have a perspective on life that is quite different from that of my friends and peers. Growing up, I often found the advice my friends were getting—*fit in, listen to adults, follow your parents' example*—was completely different from the advice my dad and mom were giving to my seven siblings and myself. My parents were teaching us to follow our own destiny, and to go within and trust our innermost voice. They were teaching us that we are all pieces of God, created with our own purpose in this world.

Recently, I wrote a letter to my father that details what being raised this way meant to me:

> *Today I sat behind you in Ephesus, Turkey, while you gave a lecture to a few hundred people who had traveled from all over the world to hear you speak. I was overcome with emotion as I saw you standing there, fulfilling your dharma while touching the lives of so many. I know you as my father, but you have always been a teacher to me as well. You have taught me that the solutions to all of life's problems are inside of me, and that*

I only had to go within, be silent and present, and know that all is well.

You never told me how to live or what to think or what to believe in. Instead, you showed me how to make each step a prayer and each word a word of love. You taught me about Rumi, St. Francis, Hafiz, Jesus, Buddha, Krishna, Mohammed, St. Germain, Neville, and so many others. You taught me to believe in magic and miracles, and you showed me how to be in awe of the awesome world we live in.

Since the time I was brought into this world, I knew that I was safe to be exactly as I was, and that whoever I was, I was a perfect creation of God. You told me that I was God and that it was God that looks out from behind my eyes. I learned from you that I was the master of my own fate, the creator of my destiny.

Of all the lessons I have learned, the thing that hit me hardest was when you said that I AM GOD. Could I really be a spark of God, a perfect creation put here on Earth with a purpose? You say this all the time, but I have always struggled with it, especially since school and society were telling me otherwise. I doubted myself, felt inferior, and worried that I needed to apologize to something for even contemplating this idea. I have felt unworthy, undeserving, and unsure. Although you gave me great tools, I still had to figure out how to use them on my own. Now I understand that God is love, God is beauty, and God is truth. You told me I came from an infinite space of perfection and that I will return to it one day, too. Slowly I am beginning to understand.

People love you so much, and yet to me you have always been Dad. You drove me to school each morning, you taught me how to swim and ride a bike, you read me stories, and you came to all my plays. As I have grown, you have encouraged me to trust my inner callings and go after whatever it is that excites me. You believe in me, Dad, and I love you so much for that.

What do you say to someone who gave you life and then showed you how to live it? You say thank you, thank you, thank you.

I realized that my experience growing up with spiritual parents was such a special one that I wanted to spread some of that wisdom to others. So I took inspiration from one of my dad's favorite sayings: *Don't die with your music still in you.* Writing this book was a way for me to do what I love most, which is telling stories—and to feel that I may be adding a little good to the world in the process.

I have structured this book in such a way that it essentially follows the *10 Secrets for Success and Inner Peace.* I respond to the teachings Dad laid out in that book, and then he adds his take at the end of each chapter. We feel this gives you a unique perspective, from both a father and a daughter, and hope you'll be able to come away with your own inspiration as well.

— **Serena Dyer**

INTRODUCTION FROM WAYNE

In the late 1990s I was being interviewed on a late-night talk show in Sydney, Australia, and I was asked a question that I pondered quite a bit before responding to the host of the show. Upon returning home, I decided to write a book that would more thoroughly and conscientiously answer what I'd been asked. The host's question had been something like, "After you have departed this earthly domain, what legacy would you like to leave for your eight children to remember you by?"

The chapters in the book I titled *10 Secrets for Success and Inner Peace* represent the fundamental truths that I attempted to live by in my role as a teacher and parent. These are the central core ideas that I have explored and lived in my many years as a writer and public speaker. These are the secrets that I believed when mastered and applied would allow my sons and daughters to truly live a life of success and inner peace.

There is a fundamental axiom that both my wife and I practiced in the raising of our children and it is this: *Parents are not for leaning upon, but rather exist to make leaning unnecessary.* Each of the ten chapter titles in my book reflects the idea that we wanted to raise self-reliant children to become successful and peaceful adults. Success was not to be measured by external indices such as how much money they made, or how far they advanced in an occupation, or how many awards they accumulated, or how they stacked up in comparison to their contemporaries. Rather, we wanted our children to value themselves, to become risk takers, to be self-reliant, to be free from stress and anxiety, to be able to celebrate their present moments, to experience a lifetime of wellness, to fulfill their own spiritual callings, to be creative—and, most significantly, to live with a sense of inner peace, regardless of any and all external circumstances.

I wrote *10 Secrets for Success and Inner Peace* so that my children would be able to have a compilation of the paramount ideas that formed the essential nucleus of my life's teaching in one place. When I gave each of them a copy, I said, "If you ever wanted to know what was most essential to me, these are the ideas that I have attempted to live by, and these are the ideas that I employed in all of my parental interactions with you throughout your life."

My daughter Serena has now responded to the book I wrote with one of her own. The title she chose is taken from one of the most profound teachings that I have applied in my own life. As I've told her very frequently, there would be no greater tragedy than if she came to the end of her life and had the realization that she didn't fulfill her own destiny.

"You came here with music to play," I told all of my children. "You don't want to ultimately realize that you didn't fulfill your own dharma because you tried to please someone else's mental picture of what you should be doing—and that includes me as your father as well." Serena has given a multitude of great examples of what it was like to be raised in a family where she did not have to live up to her parents' notion of what was best for her (or any of her siblings).

Throughout her life, Serena has always been perplexed by the frequently asked question, "What was it like to have Wayne Dyer as your father?" With this book, she has done a masterful job of not only answering that question, but of also providing guidelines to readers for living the principles outlined in its pages. At the end of each of Serena's chapters, I offer my own personal reaction to all that she has written.

I couldn't be more proud of Serena for taking on this mighty task of writing a book, and doing it with honesty and fearlessness. I know you will find it as informative and inspiring as I have.

— I AM,
Wayne W. Dyer

CHAPTER 1

DON'T DIE WITH YOUR MUSIC STILL IN YOU

*"There is no greater gift you can give or receive
than to honor your calling. It's why you were born.
And how you become most truly alive."*

— OPRAH WINFREY

I was raised with the idea that each of us has our own "music"—that we live in a perfect universe, where everything is connected, and every one of us is here for a purpose. Each of our souls will learn lessons and teach others; that's why we come to this planet. I've never doubted that I showed up here with a mission, but the mission itself has not always been clear.

Don't die with your music still in you is the most profound phrase I heard over and over as a child. I knew that we all incarnated in this lifetime with a purpose, with something unique that called to us and excited our soul, and the idea of dying without ever expressing the music I came here to play terrified me. It still does! I've asked myself many times what my purpose is—why am I here?

As a child, my parents instructed me not to follow the crowd. "Try not to get caught up in what other people tell you to do," they would say. "Just follow your heart, Serena."

Later, when I was a teen, they'd tell me, "When you follow the herd, you're bound to step in shit. Avoid the herd. Think for yourself. Do what you feel is right for you."

I heard this kind of thing all the time, but it wasn't exactly easy to take such advice. Doing what I wanted and doing what was right were often not the same thing. I wanted to try drugs, to drink alcohol with my friends, to party and lie to my parents about it. I knew that these things were not "right," but I also knew that they were what I wanted to do. I would often justify my behavior by telling myself that it was the right thing to do because I had a desire to do it—I was just following my heart. But you know what? I did these things and learned from them, and now I hardly think about them. The times in my life when I didn't make the best choices were often times of great struggle that led to enormous personal growth. I try not to judge my past; after all, I wouldn't be who I am without it!

I know that not dying with your music still in you isn't about what you "do with" your life. It is about how you *lead* your life. Raising children to dance to the beat of their own drum means raising them first to hear, and then to follow, their own inner calling. It means encouraging them to follow their hearts—to listen to their intuition, and nothing else. It also means encouraging them to move forward in their lives, rather than keeping them stuck on a decision they made in the past.

Being yourself allows you to enjoy every step of your journey, without ever having to change for someone else. As I get older, I understand that life really is about the journey. While that once irked me, I now love it!

Showing Us the Way

I think my parents knew that the best way to teach their children how to be true to themselves was to model it—and that's exactly what they did. For example, my dad never dressed the way other fathers did. People used to send him T-shirts in the mail with all kinds of sayings on them, and he wore those T-shirts every day of my childhood. I remember I begged my parents to let me take cotillion (an etiquette and dance school for kids), and when it came time for the father/daughter dance, all the fathers showed up in tuxedos. My dad, on the other hand, wore khaki pants, Birkenstocks, and a T-shirt that said IMAGINE ALL THE PEOPLE LIVING LIFE IN PEACE. It wasn't that he was trying to be rebellious; he just didn't own a suit!

Mom and Dad also followed their own path in terms of their relationship. They didn't get married until they were pregnant with me—and I'm the sixth out of eight children! I asked my mom why they got married at that point, and she said it was because that's when they both felt inclined to do so. (Personally, I think it was God's way of preparing them for the child who was on the way—me. If they hadn't been married before I was born, surely one of them would have run for the hills after!)

One of the early memories I have of dancing to my own beat took place when I was very young, in first or second grade. We were being taught in religion class that only those who have been baptized and believe in Jesus as their savior make it to heaven. I raised my hand and asked, "But what if they live somewhere really far away where no one knows about Jesus? How could that be their fault? How could God not take them to heaven if it wasn't their fault?"

My teacher gave a vague answer that didn't really address my growing concern for these souls who weren't going to get to heaven. I kept pressing it, insisting that God would surely allow a little child who had never met any Christians or heard about Jesus into heaven. It seemed obvious to me that someone so young couldn't be to blame for their lack of knowledge about Jesus. When my teacher rigidly responded that she believed you had to be baptized and accept Jesus as your savior in order to go to heaven, I recall feeling so bad for her that she thought God's love was insensitive and, even worse, intolerant.

A few years later, a similar thing happened. We were studying current events in sixth grade, and the topic of the week was immigration. To my surprise, the majority of my class believed that people who were not born in American should be "sent back to their own countries." I remember saying something like,

"But what if these people were brought here when they were babies and America is all they know? What if they work really hard and contribute to our society? Shouldn't they have a chance to stay? Aren't we all children of immigrants in this country?" I went to a Christian school, and was incredibly upset that my classmates had so little compassion. I was so distraught that I actually started to cry—really hard—in front of the whole class. Even though it would have been easier to sit quietly and "go with the herd," I just couldn't keep quiet.

When I got home from school and told my parents about these distressing experiences, they told me how proud they were of me. They congratulated me for being curious and not backing down when a teacher told me an answer that felt unacceptable to me.

Typical parental instructions like, "Be like everybody else," "Try to be normal," and "Just try fitting in" were never spoken in my home. Instead, Mom and Dad were the weirdos who were always telling my brothers and sisters and me that fitting in was unnecessary, and that some rules are meant to be broken.

My parents taught me to trust my own desires, listen to my heart, and follow what I knew to be right for me. They encouraged me to abandon any beliefs on religion that didn't feel right to me, and to let go of any beliefs about society that didn't resonate with me. They clearly agreed with Albert Einstein, who reportedly once said that "common sense is the collection of prejudices acquired by age 18." They felt that sometimes it was best not to use common sense, but to use intuition instead.

Whenever my siblings and I argued, Dad would repeat the Native American saying, "No tree has branches so foolish as to fight amongst themselves." He would say that we are all branches on the tree of humanity, so fighting was pointless. For a while I thought he was insane, but today it makes sense. I find that this saying can also apply to our relationships with ourselves.

When we hide who we really are in order to fit in or belong, we are suffocating our souls. Our true calling may pass us by while we're trying make other people happy. And if we don't love our bodies, it's because we don't understand that the body is just a vessel to contain the soul. Eckhart Tolle says, "You are the universe, expressing itself as a human for a little while." Having an internal battle where we hate our bodies or reject who we really are has the same effect as two branches of a tree fighting amongst themselves. We cannot experience peace if our inner dialogue is always at war with itself. Over time I have learned that a mind at war with itself—which is another way of saying a mind that rejects its true calling, its own nature and body—is a mind that cannot experience eternal gentleness.

If your inner dialogue is constantly telling you what is wrong with you or your life, I suggest observing that little voice without attachment to what it is saying. For me, I am able to quiet my own inner dialogue by meditating. For others, going for a run, listening to their favorite music, or doing yoga is effective. Do whatever works for you!

The Power of Intuition

As I was growing up, some of my friends' parents seemed to be concerned with what grades my friends were getting, what colleges they were applying to, and what jobs they were going to get. My own parents were nothing like this. I often wondered how I would feel if my mother and father told me where to go to school or what kind of career to pursue. Would I like it? Would it feel like too much pressure? Or would it actually make decisions easier?

The whole idea was so foreign to me. Dad had always told my siblings and me that our *dharma* (a Sanskrit word which basically means your passion or calling in life) was ours alone. Our future was not for anyone else to decide—including him!

Yet as I got older, I sometimes wished that my parents would just tell me what to do. I wanted them to sit with me and go over my list of pros and cons, guiding me toward the right decision. I wished that they'd get mad at me for quitting something I'd started —that they'd force me to stick with it, or push me to try harder. At times, following my own path seemed more challenging than being told what to do. It could seem as if so much love and support and understanding made it easy for me to do nothing, which didn't make me feel good or on track.

My dad used to tell my siblings and me that we should strive to be our own boss, so I have generally shied away from any job that involves a boss—which involves basically every job I ever thought about getting! What I know now is that he was most definitely not encouraging us to refrain from getting a job altogether; he was encouraging us to work toward having a career where we could be our own boss, even if it meant starting out working for someone else.

Today, I am grateful that I struggled to figure out what to do with myself, because the struggle itself helped me to understand the direction I wanted to go. If I had been listening to others, I wouldn't have been able to develop my own sense of self, or such a strong relationship with my intuition. I now understand that when I follow my heart, I am following my intuition. My intuition and my heart are always in agreement.

I think I learned this most vividly when I was 12 years old. I was at my friend Courtney's house for a sleepover. Her brother, who was five years older than we were, was having a party at the house. Since their parents were home and everything was pretty tame, we were allowed to be downstairs "watching" the older kids hang out. (Much to the brother's annoyance, I should mention.)

My friend and I wanted to impress the older kids so badly that we were afraid to say very much out of fear we'd embarrass ourselves. At one point I went upstairs to use the bathroom, and afterward I went into Courtney's room to put on more lip gloss. As I walked inside, I heard a voice tell me to lock the door. It was a voice I'd heard before—nowadays I'd call it my intuition. Even though I was young, I knew to listen to it. But before I could get over to the door, two older guys came in. I didn't recognize them from downstairs, so I felt afraid as they closed the door behind them. One of them approached me and said it was okay, that he was a nice guy who just wanted to do something that would feel really good for me. He came over and put his hand under my shirt, touching my stomach and slowly moving upward toward my training bra. He kept saying it was going to feel good, but already I felt sick inside.

My intuition urged me to run. For a split second I worried that if I did, they wouldn't think I was "cool." But my heart and intuition were screaming that I needed to get out of there, and thank goodness I listened. I pushed the guy away and ran down the stairs to tell Courtney what had happened. I was embarrassed about it, so I asked her not to tell anyone else and she agreed. It was our secret for many years.

While I was able to escape before anything really terrible happened, the feeling of what might have been has stuck with me. Now that I'm a woman in my 20s, of course I know how things could have ended up, and I am so grateful to my little 12-year-old self for getting out of there. I think that there are situations like this that happen for all of us, and at some point, we learn to follow our intuition because we realize that it never leads us astray.

Where Passion and Purpose Meet

I've always had strong likes and dislikes, and I've always had things I am passionate about. The older I've gotten, the easier it has been to accept that certain things come preprogrammed. The problem comes when we ignore who we truly are and convince ourselves we're something we're not in the attempt to fit in.

In my younger years I tried very hard to turn my back on almost everything that came naturally to me. I loved singing and acting, for instance, but I felt nervous and embarrassed as a kid whenever I would tell someone that I took singing lessons or was in acting class. I found the things that were inherently true about myself to be embarrassing, as if they weren't good enough.

In the same way, I rejected the part of me that wanted to get married and have children. Instead, for a while I pretended as if I wanted to pursue an intellectual career and focus on that, leaving children to a later date. This is the opposite of how I actually feel—I want children *yesterday.* But I pretended that part of myself didn't exist. I claimed to believe that women who were stay-at-home moms were weak, when I actually wanted to be one of them myself!

On so many different levels, I spent much of my life ashamed of parts of myself that made me who I was. Outwardly I appeared to be in love with who I was, but inside I was very hard on myself. Of course, I was not raised this way; my parents did a wonderful job of loving me unconditionally. But I couldn't offer that same kind of love toward myself. It's as if I was focused on punishing myself for the crime of just existing as Serena—for having my own feelings and desires—that I would do things I didn't really want to do. In fact, it is only recently that I've stopped trying to turn myself into something that I am not.

I feel as though I have now finally stopped running from who I am. Today I can honestly say that I have begun a real love affair with myself. I have stopped caring about what other people think, or whether I am fitting in or not. For the first time in my life, I feel as though I am really on the path I am meant to be on.

I have watched so many of my friends struggle with doing what they are passionate about, versus doing what their families and society tell them to do. I have seen friends give up the major they wanted to study in school to pursue what their guidance counselor tells them will guarantee them a job—whether they were interested in it or not. I relate to this so much! I had a college professor once say to me, "Serena, you have a lot of potential. Don't waste it by getting married and having kids." I actually agreed with him! Today I would have a very different response, but back then I was more worried about looking right than speaking my truth.

I know so many people in their 20s who are miserable because they're pretending to be someone else, following someone else's rules and neglecting their real passions. Some of my friends assure me they will start their dream jobs later in life—that they have plenty of time. Yet I know from personal experience that whenever we conform to externally imposed expectations, we lose sight of our individual passion and purpose. Some people end up struggling their entire lives with trying to find their purpose. The good news is that if we adhere to what we're passionate about, and really believe in ourselves and the path we're on, our purpose naturally makes itself known.

I've always known what I am passionate about, but for a long time I didn't think it "counted." It doesn't fit into a neat little box called "medicine" or "science" or "math" or "building." What I am passionate about is *people.* I love connecting with others and telling stories. I am passionate about the world—about the cultures and human beings that make our planet so fascinating. And I am passionate about talking to and being in front of an audience.

As I have learned to start honoring my passions, the universe has presented me with all green lights. I grew up hearing that we are all energy, and energy is vibration. So when we make ourselves a vibrational match to whatever it is we're passionate about, the universe can't help but provide it for us. As my friend and teacher Gabrielle Bernstein explains, "We are always manifesting. Each thought we have creates an energy flow within and around our physical being. This energy attracts its likeness. So if you're thinking, *I suck,* then your energy kinda, well, sucks—and you attract sucky experiences."

I have noticed many of my friends struggling and unhappy, just as I have been so many times before. Many end up on medication, feeling that life is too much to handle without support. In some cases antidepressants and other medications can be helpful; I know people who have found great benefit in using them for a short period of time. However, it's my belief that over the long term these drugs interfere with the natural chemistry of the body—and maybe with our life's purpose as well. Many of my peers also use antidepressants and ADHD medications to get rid of a hangover or to eat less. I have done both at times, but it never felt right for me. When I feel the lowest, I have learned that I can immediately make myself feel better by serving others. I know this sounds cheesy, but it's true!

The question *What's in it for me?* has often crept into my psyche. My parents have taught me that this is the mantra of the ego. The ego is most concerned with itself; how much it can get out of something. The mantra of God—and the mantra of our higher selves—is *How may I serve?* I heard my parents say this frequently, but I never really believed them until I tried it for myself. The irony is that once I really started to practice serving others, all the things I thought I needed in life just started to show up. When I was focused on acquiring more, I always felt lacking. When I shifted my focus toward how I could serve, the money, health, and relationships I had been looking for all just started appearing in my life.

If you would like more love in your life, then I suggest you begin to offer love to people in your life that may really need a little extra of it. Do unto others as you would have others do unto you—it is that simple. When you shift your focus to how you may serve, the universe shifts its focus to how it may serve you as well. And when you are true to yourself, the universe will continue to support you on your path.

The Career Dilemma

When I was a child, Mom and Dad continually encouraged me to follow the notes of my own music. I was never criticized, even if I went after something and then abandoned it later. There were many ideas that I tried out for a while and then left behind. Yet I never felt like a failure for wanting to try something new. My parents actually encouraged me to try everything—if it didn't work out, that was okay. Dad would remind me to trust that I would eventually find my own path. He said as long as I remained passionate about what I was doing, I was moving in the right direction.

When I was 22, my best friend, Lauren, and I decided to create a television show based on our mutual love of cooking and entertaining. We came up with recipes, had a great idea for a show, and then hired a film crew to film a pilot. The idea was that we'd pitch it to the Food Network or something like that. My dad wrote me a note that I carry around with me to this day:

In case you can't read it, the note says: "Serena My Love! I believe in your show. It will work—hold the vision—this is an investment in you and your passion! I love you, Dad."

After a few months of trying to get the pilot off the ground, nothing was coming to fruition. Lauren and I both recognized that we really didn't want to do a cooking show and had just been going with the momentum of having a new idea we liked. Even though I let go of the show, I saved the note my dad had given me. I knew what he'd written applied to anything I tried in my life. It wasn't just about the TV-show idea; it related to any project or plan I would ever undertake. He believed in me! It was as simple as that. He was proud of me no matter what.

My parents' support of me has continued to carry me closer to my music. In my early 20s, I tried out several different careers. I considered becoming a professor, a chef, and an actor. None of them quite fit. The only thing I knew for sure was that I liked having an audience and working with people. So I decided I would become a lawyer! I have always been a bit on the dramatic side, and I love telling stories. Couple that with the fact that I do well in school, and I decided that I'd come up with a great idea.

Three weeks into law school, I knew I had made a huge mistake.

I'd been miserable from day one. I would sit in the parking lot before class in tears. It wasn't about the work, as I already had a master's degree and knew what hard work was all about. It was that I was beginning to understand what it actually meant to be a lawyer. It meant a lot of paperwork and a lot of detail—neither of which I was particularly good at. I also knew I did not want to be personally responsible for someone else's settlement, divorce, conviction, or acquittal. I realized the job was just not for me. Yet I felt ashamed of the thought of quitting, so I told myself I was going to stick it out for the next three years because quitting was worse than having a job you hate. (Now *that's* a piece of advice I wouldn't give my worst enemy.)

I kept going for a few more weeks; then, not surprisingly, I got physically ill. I came down with pneumonia and had to stay home from class. I will never forget Dad calling and asking me if I thought that maybe I got pneumonia because I was doing something every day that I hated. I knew he was right, but I still had too much pride to make a change. My ego was telling me that being sick and hating what you're doing were still better than quitting. So once I recovered, I went right back to school.

I'll never forget the morning I came to my senses. I was sitting in the parking lot getting ready to go into class when it hit me. *I don't have to do this.* There was no pressure from my family or my peers, no judgment about my decision one way or the other. The only person pressuring me was *me*. I text messaged my dad right then. I was still feeling ashamed, so I asked him what he would think of me if I quit.

His response was such a relief. "I am proud of you no matter what you're doing," he wrote. "If you are unhappy and getting sick over it, then leave. You will find your path, Serena, stop worrying. I love you." Reading this, and talking to my mom later, I felt safe to follow my heart. I knew they were proud of me no matter what I was doing. I let go of the self-imposed guilt and shame, and my law school days were over.

No Such Thing as Failure

My dad used to say that some people live their entire lives pretending to be something they're not, or pretending to love something they don't, only to wake up one day and realize that they haven't really lived. This reminds me of the book *The Death of Ivan Ilyich* by Leo Tolstoy. As Ivan is dying, he asks himself, "What if my whole life has been wrong?" When I read that, I remember thinking that no matter what, I wasn't going to choose that fate.

I had been taught to listen to my own calling, to ignore what anyone else said, and to follow my own music. And yet I'd tried to convince myself to stay in law school out of fear of being criticized—when I myself was my own greatest critic! Eventually I realized I would never be at peace if I didn't follow my own heart. I knew I was doing what looked right rather than what *felt* right. I had to look at myself in the mirror each night, knowing I was abandoning myself. Slowly, I began to understand that it wasn't about what other people would think. What was important was what *I* thought.

Dad has often talked about how in his personal life, great transformation has usually been preceded by a great fall. To that end, it was only after he forgave his alcoholic father for abandoning him that he was able to write *Your Erroneous Zones*, which has sold over 70 million copies worldwide to date. J.K. Rowling, the author of the Harry Potter books, said that "rock bottom became the solid foundation on which I rebuilt my life." It was only when she got to rock bottom that she was able to make her way back up, and look how far she's come!

My husband, Matt, is a successful businessman who prides himself on his number of failures. This may sound odd, but as he puts it, "You can't put a price tag on those failures because of the valuable lessons they taught me." Matt says that whenever he enters into a somewhat risky business deal, he remains unattached to how it will turn out. He knows that, successful or not, the deal will give him experience, so he'll gain something either way. I now view the rejections of my own inner calling in the same light. I can't put a price tag on how valuable those lessons were for me, because if I hadn't rejected myself and ignored my inner voice in so many different ways, I may still be doing it today!

It seems to me that fear is what stops most of us from playing our own music. It was definitely true for me—I was afraid of letting people down, of what other people might think of me, of what I would do if I left law school and how that would look. Perhaps you're afraid that if you make a change you'll let people down, but take the risk and see what happens. You may let people down and you may not. You'll probably be pleasantly surprised by how it all turns out.

According to *A Course in Miracles*, there are only two basic emotions: fear and love. When you decide to play your own music, you are acting out of love for yourself and your own unique path. I know that when I'm living from love rather than fear, I never fail.

I was raised to understand that failure is an illusion, anyway. No one fails at anything. Everything you or anyone else does produces a result. Dad sometimes uses the analogy of playing catch. If he throws a ball to me and I drop it, I didn't fail—I just produced an unexpected result! Dad taught me that failure is just a judgment, and it is a judgment based in fear. The real question, he would say, is what do you do with the result? Do you complain about not being able to catch the ball? Or do you see it as a learning experience, saying "Throw it again!" until you succeed?

My sister Tracy is a great example of what I'm talking about here. Tracy was in her 30s and working as an executive for Best Buy (a large electronics retail corporation) in Minneapolis, and although she was very successful, she didn't feel fulfilled. She decided to follow Dad's advice and left her position to pursue her real passion, which is designing purses. My sister went from working at a corporation and having insurance, benefits, and a retirement plan to being totally on her own—having to figure out how to get her bags made and sold around the country.

Although there were bumps in the road, Tracy now sells handbags that use recycled water bottles in the manufacturing process. What's more, she managed to combine her understanding of technology from working at her former position at Best Buy with her love of design. Now she has an amazing and successful line of purses called Urban Junket that can actually charge your phone or computer! My sister had to face her fear of failure and take a leap of faith. But because she was willing to take the risk, she's now doing what she always dreamed about.

When we let ourselves be guided by love—love for ourselves, love for others, and love for what we do—fear cannot survive. As the poet Rudyard Kipling once wrote: "If you can meet with Triumph and Disaster / And treat those two imposters just the same; / Yours is the earth and everything that's in it."

Triumph and disaster are imposters. They are not real; they exist only in your mind. Fear is the same. Think of how many things you may have feared as a child that now seem silly. To be afraid of following your dreams may seem just as funny to you once you have faced it. Just think how great it will be to be doing what you love and to look back and think how silly it was to be so fearful. I know that's how I feel about leaving law school. Looking back, I can't believe I allowed myself to get so sick over it! Instead, I've discovered a whole new and better world by finding—and following—my dharma.

Finding Your Own Dharma

Shortly after leaving law school, I attended a three-day conference in Maui that my dad was putting on. Sitting in the audience, I kept contemplating the idea of my own dharma. What was it that I really wanted to do with my life?

While sitting there, I was struck with the idea that I wanted to bring the message I was raised on to people my own age. I wanted to help those who were struggling to find their place in the world, just as I had been. I asked Dad how he felt about my writing a book based on his work, and he thought it was a great idea. Shortly after that, I called Reid Tracy, the CEO of Hay House, and pitched the idea to him. Reid thought it sounded great, too. I started to feel like I was really moving on my correct path. The universe kept sending me "You go, girl!" signals that let me know I was heading in the right direction. Now I can say that writing this book has been one of the most important and fulfilling experiences of my life. Today, I am writing and speaking and moving in the direction that feels most natural and peaceful to me. I am doing it all with confidence.

The truth is, it's not where you are, it's the direction you're heading in. As a Turkish proverb says, "No matter how far you have gone on a wrong road, turn back." For me, law school was the wrong road. But by following my heart, I was able to turn around. All it took was to trust that it would all work out. Now, I know that's not as easy as it sounds. Believe me, there were many nights when I would lie awake worried about what I was going to do with my life. My ego was definitely bruised, especially when I had to tell people that I was leaving, but I let that go as well. Parts of me still believed that my image was everything, and if I wasn't "doing something" I was a failure.

I've finally realized that it doesn't matter what you are or aren't doing. It only matters whether you're moving in the direction that feels right to you, regardless of what others might think.

There's something I have heard my father say too many times to count: "You will never regret what you do in life; you will only regret what you don't do." Everything I have ever done has taught me something, whether it worked out or not. Sometimes the take-away is simply knowing what I *don't* want.

So if there's one piece of advice I'd give you, it's to notice whether you are moving toward or away from what excites you. If you're repeating the same bad habits and continuing to let yourself down by being unwilling to make a shift or change, then you're moving away from what excites you. On the other hand, if you're willing to let go of what you know is harmful for you, and willing to change your beliefs about yourself in order to get what you want in life, then you'll be moving toward what excites you. If you pay attention and let yourself be guided by your intuition, you won't have to worry about dying with your music inside of you.

The Courage to Change

In the past few years, my mom has injured herself more than she has in all the other years of her life combined. She has broken her collarbone, cheekbone, and foot; has had pins and needles put in her elbow and shoulder after falling headfirst down a spiral staircase; and, most recently, suffered a third-degree burn on her wrist. My parents are no longer together (more on that later) but they are still very close friends who speak every day, so Dad asked Mom if she thought there might be an emotional component to all of her injuries. At first she was defensive and said of course not—she was just getting older and had some early-onset osteoporosis due to having so many children.

Shortly after this, my mom and I were making dinner alone together before the rest of the family arrived for the meal. She told me that what Dad had said about her injuries really bothered her, but she couldn't stop thinking about it. She went on to say that she felt really stuck in her life at this time, and it was if she were standing on the edge of a road that had two paths. One path was starting a new life for herself, serving her own highest calling now that her children had grown and were out of the house. The other path was one of getting older and possibly getting sick and leaving this planet.

Mom has been a mother for the past 41 years and has been incredibly devoted, loving, and nurturing in the process. Her whole life had been wrapped up in raising her children, and now that she wasn't doing that so much anymore, she felt that she had other work that needed to be done and couldn't ignore it any longer. She explained that she felt an inner calling to write and teach about childbirth and raising children in a natural way, but she'd always been afraid of doing that work because she didn't feel worthy of it.

Hearing her tell me this, I was so astonished. Mom is the most worthy woman in the world of teaching about motherhood and childbirth, and yet she doubted her own true calling. She believed in me my entire life and encouraged me to do anything and everything I could dream of, but she didn't feel deserving of the very things she'd always offered me! The funny thing was that I could relate to not feeling worthy of honoring "real" dreams and instead choosing to do something else or nothing entirely. So many of us appear to have it all together, but inside we are rejecting our true desires on a massive level.

I knew that my mother had started writing a book on childbirth, and her dream was to finish it and start to teach and lecture on the subject matter. Since I'd just finished working on my own book with a wonderful editor, Kelly Notaras, I told Mom that whatever she had written up until that point was enough. She needed to e-mail Kelly right then and there and set up a time to talk so that they could begin to work together.

My mom was really hesitant and said that she needed more time. I put down the food I was preparing, and I looked her in the eye and said that I needed her to finish her book and begin doing the work she felt called to do because I needed her to *live*.

With tears in her eyes, she said okay and walked over to her iPad. She sent Kelly an e-mail that said she was "sick of my own excuses" and was ready to leave her fear behind. In her, I could recognize the very thing I felt in myself when I had made a similar decision years before in my life. Mom was so emotional about it because she made the choice to honor her calling, her passion, her dream—and in doing so, she was flooded with relief and pride. I don't know if I have ever been more proud of her, because I know what a challenge that can be.

We went back to cooking, and I noticed that my mom kept checking her iPad to see if she had any new e-mails. About an hour later she exclaimed, "She wrote back!" Mom then read Kelly's e-mail out loud to me, which basically said that she'd be happy to work with my mother on her book, and Mom began to cry. She told me that she felt proud of herself, *really* proud of herself, and she felt so much relief just by sending that first e-mail!

Making the choice not to die with our music inside of us can be gut-wrenchingly hard, but it is so worth it.

WAYNE'S RESPONSE

There is a reason that Serena picked the title of this chapter to be the title of her book. Put simply, there is no greater lesson for us to understand in this journey we call our life. I have persistently emphasized to my children, and to myself as well, that we come to this earth for a brief parenthesis in eternity for a reason. And staying aligned with what feels like our purpose is the key to living a fully functioning life, day in and day out.

My children heard me emphasizing this point over and over throughout all of their lives: "There are no accidents in the universe, and that includes you and all that you were meant to experience and accomplish as well." To me it is simply the only logical conclusion. If there is intelligence behind life, and there is every reason to believe that there must be, then *all* of that intelligence is innate in each creation of that intelligence. The source of all life is complete and entire within each of us. "All you have to do," I would tell my children (and myself), "is to discover it for its power and perfection to be *yours*."

Even our most erudite scientific scholars acknowledge the existence of a conscious and intelligent mind that is the matrix of all matter. It matters not what we call this source; all we really need to be assured of is that there is no place that it is not, and therefore it is within us to discover and apply it in all the days of our lives. Mark Twain described the significance of this awareness in this way: "The two most important days in your life are the day you were born, and the day you find out why." Serena writes passionately in this chapter about this idea, reminding us that no one can find their purpose by attempting to be just like everybody else, or to attempt to live out someone else's idea of what that purpose ought to be.

I have always taught that the purpose of life is to live a life of purpose. This means learning to tame the demands of the ego and to listen to a new inner mantra that quietly reminds us to focus on "How may I serve?" as opposed to "What's in it for me?" I spoke frequently to all of my children about the importance of trusting their own intuition, which is really the voice of God nudging them in the direction of their own highest aspirations. I would remind them that when they completely trusted in themselves, with no fear of failing or outside judgments, they were actually trusting in the very wisdom that created them. I would remind Serena frequently that all she had to do was to be herself, which is a Divine creation, and that what others thought of her was really none of her business. "You came here with your own music to play," I would tell her over and over. "And you only have a short time here to fulfill your own unique dharma. No one can do it for you, and it is impossible for you to fail at being yourself."

I love the sound of the words *Don't die with your music inside you*. It is such a powerful reminder that we all came here with some kind of music to play; it has to be true in a universe that is guided and directed by an invisible supreme intelligence at the helm. This was a message that all of my children heard frequently.

I have often used these words of the great poet Kahlil Gibran from his timeless tome, *The Prophet:*

> *Your children are not your children.*
> *They are the sons and daughters of Life's longing for itself.*
> *They come through you but not from you,*
> *And though they are with you, yet they belong not to you.*

I learned to understand and apply the significance of this message. My children all came here to play their own music, and I did not want to be a person who would stifle or silence that urge with them, simply because I happened to be their father.

Serena's stories in this chapter reflect the value that my wife, Marcelene, and I placed on allowing our children to fulfill their own callings. Both Marcie and I knew very early on that our role was to unpretentiously guide, then step aside. No one could be more proud of Serena and all of her siblings than her parents, who know the mighty truth hidden in the title of this chapter and this book itself. We do not want to have our sons and daughters arrive at the end of their lives and utter those infamous words of Ivan Ilyich, "What if my whole life has been wrong?"

CHAPTER 2

Have a Mind That Is Open to Everything and Attached to Nothing

"The measure of intelligence is the ability to change."
— ATTRIBUTED TO ALBERT EINSTEIN

My mom always says that she had the most overwhelming sense of peace when she was pregnant with me. That's why she named me Serena. Yet shortly after I was born, my parents joked that they should have named me Storm, since I was constantly crying and always unhappy. After a few months, they actually started to worry about me. The doctors were worried as well, because I had only gained about seven ounces in the first six months of my life. There was talk that I may not make it.

I am the sixth of eight children. My older siblings are Tracy, Shane, Stephanie, Skye, and Sommer; after me came Sands and Saje. By the time I arrived, given that my parents were well versed in child rearing, they were very familiar with the cries of a baby. They knew if it was a hungry cry, a stinky-diaper cry, or a hurt cry. Mom says that the cry I made was different—it was one of terror. Every time she laid me down in my crib, I started screaming. I also kept my fists balled up, as children often do when they're experiencing stress or fear, but this was a constant state for me.

My mother decided to wear me in a sling around the clock in order to ease my constant tension. Luckily for all of us, it worked.

By the time I was two, my parents were aware that I was different from my brother and sisters. I was extremely sensitive to both touch and sound. I would rock back and forth, sometimes for hours, not letting anyone touch me. I'd get upset when certain things went against my skin. I would hide food—in my crib, in my diaper, in drawers around the house—and when my mom would find it and try to throw it away, I'd scream and cry. I was terrified by loud noises. Anytime a plane was flying overhead, I would run, hide, and scream. And what I screamed were the words *Hey, phone!*

This wasn't the only strange thing I would say. My parents heard me shouting out indecipherable words and phrases in my sleep many times. Not knowing what to think, they chalked it up to jibber jabber—just one more aspect of my bizarre behavior. Eventually, doctors told my parents that I was possibly exhibiting some early signs of autism.

Years before all of this, my dad had counseled a couple with a severely autistic son. This young boy, Raun, would rock himself back and forth for hours and had no emotional contact with anyone, including his parents. His parents, Barry "Bears" and Samahria Kaufman, had decided to go against everything Raun's doctors were telling them to do—they decided to dedicate their time and energy toward showering their son with love and acceptance every minute of the day. As their counselor, Dad had encouraged their efforts, even though he had no idea what the outcome would be. My father has always believed in keeping his mind open to everything and attached to nothing, meaning open to new ideas but unattached to the outcome. He really respected this couple for being open to the possibility of healing their son, while remaining unattached to the outcome.

Thanks to his parents' unconditional love and support—and their willingness to remain open to everything—Raun emerged from the other world he was living in and became a "normal" young man in every sense of the word. The Kaufmans went on to create the Son-Rise Program® (www.autismtreatmentcenter.org), which has helped tens of thousands of families around the world based on the work they did with their own son.

When I began exhibiting some of the same behaviors that Raun displayed, Dad and Mom remembered what the Kaufmans had done and decided to take a similar approach with me. They called everyone in our family into a meeting and explained their intention to have me feel loved, wanted, and embraced no matter what type of odd behavior I was exhibiting. If I had an outburst and was screaming and shaking, my parents never yelled at me, grabbed me, or punished me. When I had a sensitivity toward something such as loud noises or airplanes, they would honor that sensitivity and comfort me, rather than force me to "get over it."

Mom and Dad used to tell my siblings and me that we "picked" them to be our parents and teach us what our soul needed to learn in this lifetime. I often think that if this is true, I am so glad I picked them because most other parents would have locked me up or ignored me for being so crazy! I can't say with 100 percent certainty that when I'm a parent, I will be as patient as they were (especially my mom). I am incredibly thankful for both of them.

The Process of Letting Go

The fear I'd been living with slowly but surely fell away, and I became a happy and bright little girl. I had emotional connections with everyone in my family, and people described me as funny and outgoing. From time to time, however, I would go back to this fearful place. These "episodes," as my parents called them, sometimes lasted for days. I would rock myself and shout out words in a language that was not my own.

One New Year's Eve I was at home with my grandmother while my parents were out to dinner with friends. The noise of fireworks set me off into one of my episodes, and I was inconsolable. My grandmother called my parents, who decided to come home and get me, thinking I might calm down if I were with my mom. My parents ended up taking me with them back to the restaurant, where I carried on in my jibber jabber there at the table. One of the members of the wait staff overheard, and with a look of amazement told my mom that I was speaking Vietnamese. My parents had both thought it sounded like I spoke an Asian language, and I appeared to be "fluent" in it—especially when I talked in my sleep. They weren't sure whether to believe the server, however, because I had never been around a Vietnamese person in my life. It certainly didn't make sense that I could have mastered a foreign language at the age of two.

My parents kept the server's words in the back of their minds, but didn't try to confirm or deny whether I was indeed speaking Vietnamese. Shortly after the incident, however, Dad was offered a reading from Lee Chang, a very popular and respected channeler in Seattle. As a writer and speaker in the spiritual world, my father is frequently offered readings and healings, and from time to time he says yes. He and Mom have always been very open, choosing to see this world as overflowing with miracles and believing that everything is possible. My parents were going to Seattle for a trip anyway, so Dad decided it would be neat to meet with Lee. Since Mom was still wearing me most everywhere at that time, they brought me along as well.

During the reading, Lee told Dad a number of personal details that she could not possibly have known. Most astoundingly, she told him that in a past life, the daughter he had with him had died tragically as a child in Vietnam. Lee said that I was still experiencing memories of being there, but eventually they would go away. Of course she had no way of knowing that someone had already told my parents I was speaking Vietnamese, nor did she know that I had been exhibiting autistic-type behaviors. All Lee Chang had seen that day was a happy, smiling little girl sitting on her mom's lap.

Lee went on to give some details of my life in Vietnam. She said I had a mother, father, and brother, and we'd all died in a bombing attack—which helped explain my fear of planes. Lee also said that I'd been very poor and often gone hungry in that life, thus my habit of hiding food.

Mom and Dad weren't sure what to make of this story. They'd heard of past lives, of course, but had never really given the idea much thought. As time went by, my episodes continued to become less and less frequent. Yet from time to time, when a really loud plane would fly overhead, I would still yell out "Hey, phone!" and try to hide. And then, when I was eight years old, I consciously allowed a part of me to let go. I remember surrendering everything I was feeling and handing it over to God. I want to mention that for me, "God" is the term that applies to the greatest good that all of us are a part of. I think of God as the most beautiful, honest, and generous energy there is.

A friend of the family had just become a network chiropractor, and he came over to our home to offer us some of his new training. (A network chiropractor is different from a regular chiropractor in that they adjust the spine using extremely gentle movements that oftentimes don't involve any "cracking" sounds or "twisting" movements.) He explained that he used strategically placed pressure to allow his patients to release pent-up emotions or traumas.

I didn't know this guy at all, and I was always really reluctant to have people touch me, but when Mom introduced us to him, for some reason I begged her to let me go first. I just remember feeling like I needed to allow him to do this work on me. Mom agreed, and I laid on the table while he applied pressure to different points on my back.

All of a sudden, I felt myself go back in time, and had a clear vision of being in a rice paddy. This sounds insane, but it's true! I was with a man, woman, and boy—they were my mom, dad, and brother in that lifetime, and I could feel how much I loved them. I started to sob. I knew I was on a table at my house, but I could also clearly see these people and feel deep emotional ties to them.

My mom wanted to pick me up, but the chiropractor stopped her. He said it takes some patients years to be able to release this sort of emotion, so she should just allow me to let it come out on my own. He applied more pressure to my back, and suddenly I experienced an overwhelming sense of peace; I felt that everything was perfect.

When I got up from the table I told Mom that I had seen a family, and that they used to be *my* family. I said we had all been standing in a field similar to one we'd seen when my parents took me on a trip to Australia and Indonesia when I was a very young child, and we were smiling.

It might seem like my parents had planted this idea in my mind, but believe it or not, they had never told me (or anyone) what Lee Chang had said all those years before. I had no reason to believe I'd had a past life with a mom, dad, and brother. And yet, this was exactly what I had seen.

After I had this vision I felt so peaceful and healed. It's hard to describe the sense of well-being I had. It was as if somehow, on a deeper level, I knew that I needed to get that out of me. I was open and willing to let it go, without ever having even known about it in the first place.

Before this experience, I used to pray at night for God to bring me back to the place that was so beautiful and peaceful, which I assume was the place where I was in between "lives," when I was actually in the direct presence of God's energy. This seems so bizarre, because I had a happy life and loved my family so much— but it was as if I had a memory of God that was so beautiful and the feeling was so good, I'd pray to go back there. After this experience, though, I don't think I prayed to go back again.

Having heard that I said "Hey, phone!" so often as a child, I did decide to look up what it meant. I discovered that the phonetic sound in Vietnamese would be *Haiphong,* which happens to be a town in North Vietnam. It was bombed by the French in 1946, as well as by the U.S. during the Vietnam War, and thousands of civilians had been killed. Haiphong also had devastating famines in the 1940s, and many people from this region died of starvation. Maybe it's a coincidence and maybe not—I'm not very concerned either way. Instead, I choose to remain open to the idea that the universe is more amazing than our wildest dreams!

Love, Honor, and Acceptance

When I was young, someone asked me if my parents were Republicans or Democrats, so I went home and asked them. My mom said she was a "breast-feeder" and didn't have time for anything else. Dad's response was a perfect example of what it means to be unattached (in retrospect, Mom's was, too—ha!). He said that he was neither. He didn't want to be labeled as one or the other because he didn't want to have to defend the party position or vote for whoever was running for that party. Instead, he said that he would cast his vote based upon who was running and with whom he generally agreed. A mind that is open to everything and attached to nothing operates just like that; it isn't blindly stuck on labels or positions for their own sake.

Whatever beliefs I developed, whichever political party I sided with, whomever I chose to date or marry—none of that concerned my parents. My life was always completely up to me. As long as my siblings and I were safe, happy, and healthy, they encouraged us to develop our own personalities, opinions, and desires.

You might imagine how freeing it was for us as children to know that we were loved regardless of our choices or our flaws. You've seen those bumper stickers that say, I AM THE PROUD PARENT OF AN HONORS STUDENT, right? Well, growing up, our family minivan had a bumper sticker that said, I AM A PROUD PARENT UNCONDITION-ALLY. This was a funny outward sign of what all eight of us knew: that our parents loved us *no matter what*. And that was the best gift they could have given us.

Had it not been for my parents, I might have been put in special schools or institutionalized when I was little, or I could've even died. That Mom and Dad have never stopped showering me with unconditional love and understanding has helped me heal on a level that is hard to explain. I know I have a purpose here on this planet. Finding that purpose may mean staying open to things that seem impossible or strange; at the same time, it means remaining unattached to the outcome.

For me, the first part is relatively simple to understand: Be open-minded. Be willing to try new things and to accept others' idiosyncrasies without judgment. This isn't always easy, and it takes practice—but I believe it is about honoring each individual's path and knowing that everyone is doing the best they can with where they are in life. When I find myself wanting to judge someone for their way of living, I try to remind myself of what Friedrich Neitszche said: "This is my way. What is your way? *The* way does not exist." When you're part of a family with eight kids, adopting this philosophy is better than always being angry with someone!

Being attached to nothing, on the other hand, is not so simple —at least not for me. When I first heard this phrase as a child, it seemed like such a foreign concept. But over the years I've come to realize that it means letting go of any preconceived beliefs or ideas we have about the way life should be, how things should go, or how others should act or live.

Being attached to nothing does not mean we have no attachments; it means we don't get caught up in the outcome of things. It's about being present in the now, knowing that there is a lesson in everything we experience in life. It means understanding that things are going to happen that are outside of our control. People are going to change; if we're lucky, *we* are going to change, too. Trying to control and manipulate life so that everything happens just the way we like it would be like trying to stop the earth from spinning on its axis. By being attached to what may or may not happen, or to the way we've always done things, we take away the great gift of living in the moment.

It has taken me a long time to understand that on Monday I might feel one way, but I can't assume I'll still feel that way on Wednesday. Because in between, there is Tuesday! And you never know what another day will bring. When I think something like *I am this way and always have been; it's just who I am, and I can't change,* I am literally limiting the experiences I can have in my life. I don't know about you, but I wouldn't allow my 15-year-old self to buy all the clothes I'm going to wear for the rest of my life. When I was 15 I was wearing tube tops as skirts! So why should I allow my 18-year-old or 22-year-old self to determine the beliefs I'm going to hold or the type of career I'm going to have for the rest of my life?

This same logic applies to relationships. Couples that get divorced and end up being friends afterward are usually couples who understand nonattachment. They get that they both changed, in directions that were no longer compatible with the person they were with.

I myself am married, but I don't know if I would have wanted to get married if I lived in a country where divorce wasn't legal. I am in love with my husband, and I want him to be the father of my children. But what if we don't feel that way at some point? I have every intention of loving him for the rest of my life, but *what if?* What if one day we no longer love each other in *that* way? Should we stay together because that's what society thinks we should do? What if he were to meet someone else and fall in love with her? I wouldn't want him to stay with me if he were in love with someone else; not for my sake, our future children's sake, or anyone else's. I only want his soul to be free to do what it came here to do, and the same with my own. Feeling that way toward Matt is the greatest love I can imagine giving him.

My best friend, Lauren, always says that at the end of her life, if she hasn't been married at least four times she will be disappointed in herself. She is (mostly) joking, but I love her belief that if she hasn't fallen madly in love with someone to the point that she wants to marry them, she hasn't allowed herself to love madly and passionately. I don't have such lofty goals—one marriage sounds fine for me—but I love hers nonetheless!

Staying Open

In our home, nothing was taboo. Because my parents had gone through the whole past-life experience with me, our family was exposed to a wide variety of topics that some people thought were weird. We talked about ghosts, time travel, outer space, and other dimensions. And when asked about reincarnation, Dad used to recite Eleanor Roosevelt's famous quote: "You know, I don't think it would be any more unusual for me to show up in another life than showing up in this one!" I now see that Mom and Dad were trying to teach us that we live in a universe where *all* things are possible. They wanted us to know we were capable of being anything we wanted; that miracles are just a natural, regularly occurring part of life.

My friends would come over and beg my mom to do a "séance" with us because she made it fun and exciting and has always had a calmness about her that makes anyone feel safe in her presence. We'd ask if ghosts were in our house, or if there was a special message for one of us. I've since discovered that some people think séances and ghosts and the like are "devil worship." I would say to them that they are the *exact* type of people who need to contemplate what it means to have a mind that is open to everything!

My siblings and I were not raised with any particular religion. Even though we went to a religiously oriented school, my parents insisted that we make up our own minds about what we believed in. One day my sister Saje came home from school and told Mom and Dad that she was always sad when she went into the chapel and saw the crosses hanging on the walls. She said she'd heard that Jesus and other men had hung on those crosses, and she didn't like it. My parents immediately made plans to move her to a school that was nonreligious, respecting her desire not to see the crosses. My parents understood that not all children are the same, so their sensitivities need to be honored. If one of your children had a sensitivity to apples, would you continue to feed him apples? In our family, emotional sensitivities were equally honored as well.

When I was about five years old I learned that hamburgers and hot dogs actually came from animals. Like a lot of children, I didn't realize that the farm animals I sang songs about ended up on my plate at night. When I learned this, I decided that I no longer wanted to eat meat. Rather than try to force me to do something I didn't want to do, my parents honored my decision. Bless her heart, Mom even made vegetarian food especially for me.

After a few years of staying really small and hardly gaining weight (if only I had that problem now), the doctor encouraged my parents to incorporate a little meat into my diet. My mom was very concerned—to the point that she decided to trick me. She asked me if I would eat meat from animals that had run around on a farm until they dropped dead; that is, they weren't killed. I agreed that I would eat "drop-dead chicken" and "drop-dead steak," and I did. Now, I'm not condoning lying to your children! I'm pointing toward the fact that my parents did not force me to eat meat; they did what they could to honor my sensitivity toward animals while safeguarding my health. To this day I don't really like to eat meat, but I definitely start to feel tired if I don't have a little bit of it in my diet. Knowing this, I choose to eat meat selectively, remaining open to the fact that sometimes my body just needs it.

Being exposed to different cultures, religious beliefs, foods, clothing habits, and types of people made me develop a sense of compassion as a child that I am very proud of to this day. I was once asked what I would consider my "secret superpower" to be, and I said that I had a great sense of compassion and felt very proud of that. In fact, I still love myself for having this quality! I credit this to my own inner development, but also to the fact that my parents exposed my brothers and sisters and me to so many things that were different from us.

When I would see images of people from different countries in my textbooks or read about different ways of living, I felt comfortable, rather than afraid or in need of condemning it because it was different. Because I was exposed to so many things as a child, I think it helped me to grow up and take an interest in things that were different, rather than judge them. As a kid I felt that by staying open to everything, I was free to grow as a person. I still feel that way. I know that I am always evolving, so I try to be less attached to the outcome and more focused on being present in the moment.

Maybe your parents were not like mine—maybe they weren't open to everything. There's no need to blame them or find fault with them. Just as parents must love their children for who they are, we as children must love our parents as well. There are things that my mom and dad have done or said that they may not be proud of, and hopefully I will learn from that and do better with my own children. And that is the point: we all hope that future generations will take the best of the last generation and use that to move forward.

If your parents have rejected you because of who you are or how you live, try to love them for that—you are where you are now because of it. You are awakening to the wisdom that is within you. Maybe your parents weren't taught that they are perfect just the way they are, either. Having a mind that is open to everything means offering that same unconditional acceptance to the people in your life that you, yourself, are seeking. Being attached to nothing means not getting hung up on whether or not you get it back from them in return. If you can, try to love them for who they are. When you operate from this higher place, the universe will offer love and acceptance back to you tenfold.

 ᴖ

I can't tell you the number of times I've been at one of Dad's talks and heard someone tell him that they hate their career but can't change it. I always stifle a giggle because I know exactly what he's going to say, since he's been saying it to me my whole life: "If you aren't willing to change your concept of yourself—what you believe to be true about yourself—then it's true; you cannot change your career. But when you're ready to dig in and find out what's *really* true about yourself, then the universe will support you in a career change."

Being open to everything means being open to your own dreams manifesting into reality. And being attached to nothing means not getting caught up with what people will think or what the outcome will be. It means allowing yourself to do what is natural for you, without judging yourself for your dreams.

34

As I've already mentioned, I wrestled with what I was supposed to be "doing" with my life. Ever since I finished school, I felt stuck and almost depressed as I tried to figure out what my job should be. My parents tried to assure me that I didn't need to put so much pressure on myself to accomplish some big career overnight. They reminded me that as long as I remained passionate about what I was doing, I'd always find my way.

Slowly, I awakened to my true purpose. I discovered that I'm most in alignment with who I am when I'm communicating; when I am sharing knowledge that inspires me. There are myriad "jobs" that could carry out this life's purpose, but what I came to realize is that my purpose is not *what* I do. It's *how* I do it. It doesn't matter the medium I choose; it only matters that I express myself. I am expressing my purpose through this book. I don't know if I will make a career out of being a writer, and it doesn't matter. Because what I've discovered is that, when you are living on purpose, the outcome doesn't matter. The only thing that matters is that your mind stays open. To everything.

Having a mind that is attached to nothing means learning to work with situations that aren't turning out as we'd want or expect. It's seeing that everything is in perfect order anyway. It's hard to see something challenging as being in perfect order, but those of us who have gone through tough times know that we'll eventually come to realize that the sun has been shining behind the clouds all along.

WAYNE'S RESPONSE

Serena's many appropriate examples throughout this chapter illustrate the significance I have always placed on the message that is inherent in the title of this chapter. One of my favorite American novelists, Edna Ferber, once observed that "a closed mind is a dying mind." As a parent, I persistently encouraged my children to have a mind that is not only open, but is alive with excitement about the endless ways one can live so as to fulfill their own destiny.

We become what we think about all day long—this is one of the greatest secrets that so many people are unaware of as they live out their life's mission. What we think about is the business of our minds. If that inner invisibleness called our mind is closed to new ideas and infinite possibilities, it is equivalent to killing off the most important aspect of our very humanity. A mind that is open and unattached to any one particular way of being or living is like having an empty container that can allow new and endless possibilities to enter and be explored.

I have always loved Mark Twain's paradoxical description of a person who has been raised to have a closed mind and attachments to a certain way of thinking and behaving: "It ain't so much the things we don't know that get us into trouble. It's the things we know that just ain't so." My wife and I wanted our children to explore and come to understand their own unlimited potential. Topics such as reincarnation, past-life recollections, network chiropractic and energy medicine, channeling, self-healing, meditation, chanting, and on and on in an infinite laundry list of "weird" ideas were all on the table for discussion and experimentation.

All of Serena's wonderful stories from the recollections of her childhood with her "strange" parents are indicative of the importance that was placed in our home on being willing to explore any and all ideas, even if they were not accepted as part of the norm. I did not want my children to think of themselves as normal or even ordinary.

Serena's early years were unlike those of any child I have even known or read about. She came here with language that would emerge while she slept, which was not the English that was spoken in our home. Her very survival depended upon her parents having a mind that was open and unattached as to how to raise this unique and challenging baby and blossoming toddler.

I knew that my experience some 15 years earlier with an infant who had been diagnosed with incurable infantile autism was also my own preparation for how to handle Serena's symptoms as they surfaced. I had my mind opened back then when I was a young college professor and practicing therapist, and it was this lack of attachment to accepted knowledge that allowed me to not only keep an open mind but to help make my struggling daughter flourish in a world that seemed so foreign and threatening to her at the time.

The more I kept an open mind to the words of Jesus, "With God, all things are possible," the more growth I would experience, and the more my children would have the opportunity to grow as well. Albert Einstein once noted that "the mind that opens to a new idea never returns to its original size." When I saw the miracle of Raun Kaufman's deliverance from a devastating prognosis, my mind was so opened that I could never return to my old ways of thinking.

This is the environment that all of our children were raised in: a place where returning to our original size was simply an impossibility.

CHAPTER 3

YOU CAN'T GIVE AWAY
WHAT YOU DON'T HAVE

*"You can get everything in life you want if you will
just help enough other people get what they want."*

— ZIG ZIGLAR

I first learned about not being able to give away what we don't
have when I was a kid. It seems pretty logical that if you don't
have something, you can't give it away. Yet although this secret
appears pretty superficial, it actually has a lot of depth to it.

One day Dad asked me if I squeezed an orange, what would
I get out of it? I responded that I would get orange juice, because
that's what was inside of an orange. He asked if my sister squeezed
the orange, what would come out? I told him that orange juice
would still come out. He asked me if I put it in a juicer, what would
I get out of the orange? Baffled by his ridiculousness, I told him
that no matter who squeezed the orange—and no matter how,
when, or where it was squeezed—orange juice would always come
out because that's what was inside.

Then he asked me if *I* were squeezed, what would come out
of me? I told him that he would get niceness, because I had nice
inside of me. (Which was half true. I knew that the other half
of the time you would get sassiness, but I didn't bother to mention that one.) Even at such a young age, I understood the point:
You can't give away what's not inside of you. If you don't have
love, you can't give love away. If you don't have anger or hate or

anxiety, you can't give them away, either. What comes out of you is not dependent on who squeezes you or how; it is only contingent upon what is inside of you. Therefore, you and only you can be responsible for this.

My younger brother, Sands, has always been one of the most lovable people I know. He is friendly, supportive of everyone he meets, and truly finds the good (or at least the humor) in everything. He is a beautiful person inside and out, and I have learned so much about being easygoing from him. My mom calls him the little Buddha, because even though he has six sisters who cause a lot of chaos, he invariably stays calm. I have an older brother, Shane, who is also very fun and laid back. But he is 11 years older than I am and didn't grow up in the midst of the younger siblings—four of whom are girls. So in some ways, Sands had it hardest.

One summer when my siblings and I were young, we got word about who our teachers were going to be for the next school year. Since five of us all went to the same school, we often had the same teachers our siblings had had the year before. So Skye was telling Sommer about the teacher she'd be getting, and in turn Sommer filled me in on my fifth-grade teacher, whom she'd just had. Saje was going into kindergarten, so all of us told her about her new teacher, too. My brother Sands was sitting there with us but didn't say anything.

Dad came over and asked, "Sands, what do you think about your teacher?"

"I don't know," he replied. "I don't think about teachers when I'm in Maui." Little seven-year-old Sands couldn't muster up an opinion about his past or future teachers. The idea of talking about them while on vacation just didn't occur to him.

Everyone in the world loves my brother because he makes people feel safe. He doesn't think about others in a judgmental way, and he certainly doesn't talk about them—not even his teachers. As a result, what Sands receives back is more people who love him, and more people who want to do things to serve him.

Sands's lovability was never more obvious than the day we all flew up to Pennsylvania for my grandfather's birthday. It was a last-minute decision to go, and while Mom was able to get seats for the youngest four of us on her flight, we were spread throughout the plane. Sommer, Saje, and I all had seats toward the back; while Mom and Sands were toward the front. Halfway through the flight, I wanted to go say hi to Mom. As I walked to her seat, I passed by my brother, who was sound asleep between two older ladies. Sands, who was 15 at the time, had his head on one woman's shoulder, and the other one was stroking his arm. I couldn't help but laugh. I said that I was his sister, and one of the ladies put her finger up to her lips to indicate I should quiet down because he was sleeping. Then she told me that she had an extra sandwich with her that she was saving for him when he woke up.

Cracking up, I went on to see my mom and tell her what had happened. She just smiled and said, "That's Sands for ya!"

I firmly believe that you get back what you put out into the world, so what you give away to others is what you can expect to get in return. Low energy attracts low energy. In this case I'm defining low energy as thoughts that involve anger, hatred, shame, guilt, and fear. These types of thoughts not only weaken you, but they attract more of these same things back to you. High-energy thoughts, on the other hand, are those of love, happiness, peace, joy, compassion, and kindness. My little brother receives great gifts from the universe time and again because he carries these uplifted thoughts within him. It sometimes seems like he is the luckiest kid in the world, but the truth is that the universe can't help but serve him because he's so full of love.

As my friend and teacher Mastin Kipp says so beautifully, "There is nothing to chase, nothing to attain, only something to become—love. This is how all obstacles vanish." Sands is a great example of a person who lives from a space of love, and because of that, he leads a very obstacle-free life.

The only way to offer more love and kindness is to start by directing those thoughts inwardly, toward yourself. At times in my life when I've felt ashamed of where I was or what I was doing, I've been far more judgmental toward those around me as well. When

I am fulfilled, on the other hand, I feel genuine excitement toward other people's happiness.

What I've noticed is that when I become more loving toward myself, I attract more love into my life. It transforms what I'm carrying around inside of me. I like to try to notice when my thoughts turn to judgment, fear, and anger, and switch immediately to thoughts of love. I repeat the words *I am love I am* over and over in my mind until I actually feel my body relax and allow love to take over. Even if I can't manage to change the negative thought, I try to love myself for noticing it in the first place—that's a start! When I work on my self-love, self-respect, and self-empowerment, I always find I have more of these things to give away to others.

Competition and Judgment

My sister Skye is like a real angel in our family. She is kind, generous, and always looks for the good in other people. My entire life, she and I have been very, very close—and very, very different. Whenever we go out to eat or shopping together, my sister knows everyone and makes a point of asking them how they are, how their child is, and what's new in their life. My mom is the same way. I, on the other hand, have a tendency to tell people I see regularly about what is new in *my* life! I somehow seem to forget to ask them what's going on in theirs.

Just like Sands, everyone loves Skye. I believe it's because my brother and sister both see the good in others and treat everyone as a friend, no matter who they are. If Skye has a judgmental thing to say about someone, I actually watch her immediately replace it with something nice—as if she is actively catching and correcting herself.

I'm inspired by my sister's example. In fact, it seems to me that, as a society, the time has come to move away from the energy of judgment and condemnation. In order to do this, the first thing we need to look at is our own insecurity. What are we all so afraid of?

We know what we're insecure about based upon how we respond inwardly and outwardly to things that are around us. For example, when I'm not feeling physically fit, I become threatened by "get in shape" magazines and other people talking about diet and exercise. But if I'm not insecure about something, the topic has no significance to me. So if someone mentioned being an only child, I'd have nothing to be threatened by because it is the furthest thing from what I am—I would be able to listen to what that person had to say about their experience and just observe without judgment.

I've been surprised by how many people have said negative things to me when I tell them I'm writing a book. I've received remarks such as, "Well, people don't buy books anymore, so good luck with that," or "Ha! Sure you are!" I've even had several people roll their eyes. Similarly, a couple of years ago I wrote an article about meeting Oprah and doing a vision board, and the article was published on HealYourLife.com. Shortly after it came out, I got an e-mail from my dad's publicist at Hay House, who told me that Oprah.com was putting my article on their website. I was over the moon, and tweeted the link and posted it on my Facebook page. Hearing that people liked my article and that some people really got a lot out of it made me feel great!

Unfortunately, though, I also received a message from someone I know who said that I was an idiot and my article was pointless. This person went on to say that it was easy for me to be generous and kind because I didn't have to work to support myself like she did. She also said that if I had to work in the business she was in and deal with what she had to deal with, I might not be so loving. That may or may not be true—but neither one of us will ever know, because I will never be in her shoes and she will never be in mine.

It's hard not to meet judgment with judgment, so I remind myself that I need to send people like this an extra amount of love. I'm not always able to do so right away; in fact, I usually need to vent a bit first. Sometimes I'll get lost having a conversation with that person in my mind, telling them to leave their negativity at the door and asking them why they can't just be supportive and happy for me. But judging them for judging me carries the same energy they just put out toward me, so eventually I come back to my practice. As hard as it is, I send them extra love—and send myself a little bit as well.

I've been thinking a lot lately about competition amongst friends and peers. We've all heard people talk about the good things that are happening for their friends as if they wished they weren't happening, right? In my view, it isn't that we don't want each other to be happy. Rather, seeing someone else's success can trigger fears about where we are in our own lives, making us worry that we're not measuring up.

Since there are six daughters in my family, we have all experienced someone coming up to one of us and saying something like, "You're all beautiful, but you are the prettiest." They mean to be nice when they say this, but I think it is bizarre and it makes me uncomfortable. What one person finds beautiful is not the same as what another finds beautiful. The last thing I want is for people to view my sisters and me in competition with one another. We aren't and never have been. We all fully support each other, and we experience one another's successes and failures as if they were our own. We were raised to support each other and really be there for each other, in a way that is not competitive, and we have chosen to live that way as adults as well.

Recently Dad gave a lecture where he explained that human beings often view the world as limited in its abundance. Because of this view, many of us think that if someone else gets something, their having it limits our ability to get it as well. It would be like me being upset because my sister got a car. I can honestly tell you that there has never been a time in my life when one of my siblings has gotten something that I didn't feel genuine happiness for them. This isn't because I'm a saint; it's because I was raised with the belief that we live in a universe where there is more than enough to go around!

The truth is, what others get or don't get has nothing to do with you. Someone becoming financially successful doesn't impede your chance of becoming financially successful, unless you believe it does. Believing that someone else's clothing line will negatively impact yours is taking the focus off of how great yours can be, and placing it on how much better theirs may be in comparison with yours. There is not only one star in the NBA—there are many stars on every team, and they all work together to make the league great. Sure, there is some competition, but at the end of the day, all of the players are working toward their common goal of focusing on being the best they can be and not worrying what anyone else in the NBA is doing.

My dad once told me that there are two ways to have the tallest building in the city. The first way is to monitor your neighbor's building, and every time they add a brick, you sneak over and take it down. The second way is to build your own, not paying attention to how tall your neighbor's building is. When you put your focus on what you want, instead of on what someone else has, you will only attract what you want into your life. If your focus is on taking someone's bricks down, on the other hand, you will never have time to work on your own building. I've found this analogy helpful in so many situations in my life.

If we are consumed with worry and judgment over what others are doing, we don't have time to work on ourselves. I'm a big fan of Jesus, and I love when he said, "He that is without sin among you, let him first cast a stone" (John 8:7). Casting the first stone is a metaphor for casting judgment on anyone. He also said, "Judge not, that you be not judged. For with what judgment you pronounce you will be judged, and with the measure you use it will be measured back to you" (Matthew 7:1–2). I believe Jesus is saying that when we cast judgment on others, we are aligning ourselves with the energy of judgment. What we'll get back is more reason for others to judge us.

Anyone who has lost a significant amount of weight will tell you that there came a point in their life where they were just sick of being overweight—and from that point forward, they were aligned with their goal of losing the weight until eventually choosing the right food and exercising regularly became their natural choice. These people had to make a conscious decision to change their habits in order to change the experience they were having in life, and I think judgment should be handled in a similar way. If we make a conscious choice to stop condemning and judging our peers, and we slowly practice it until it becomes second nature, we will find that the judgment we receive has lessened as well. Or we just won't care about it anymore. Either way, it sounds nice to me!

Finding God Within

Many people were raised to think that God is outside of us—that God is separate and to be feared. I was raised to think the opposite. My parents taught me that God is peering out from behind my eyes, and that it's my job here on Earth to live from a space of God's love. It isn't so much about being positive as it is about being grateful.

It recently hit me during a yoga class that the one attitude I try to maintain is that of gratitude. I think that optimism and gratitude go hand in hand in a spiritual sense. To be optimistic is to be hopeful and positive about the future, while to be grateful is to *know* that whatever you are going through or have experienced has been designed to teach you something you needed to learn. It seems to me that optimism is the hope that everything will work out, and gratitude is the absolute knowing.

Gratitude is the knowing that everything is in perfect, Divine order, even on the darkest days of our lives. Gratitude is not the *hope* that it will all work out; it's being thankful that it already has. Even when things don't end up as we expected or prayed they would, we can still hold on to the knowing that there is a bigger picture and something to learn from the experience. Whatever our circumstances, everything is part of a Divine plan that's bigger than we can even imagine.

Gratitude is truly about treasuring our own magnificence. I believe we are all a part of God, and that together, we *are* God. When we send hate and fear toward others, we are sending that energy toward God, toward one of His own perfect creations. We aren't serving our own highest self—the piece of us that *is* God.

It's my belief that we must come to a place where we know that God does not exist outside of us, but within us. My dad taught me that in the Bible, Moses is asked by a burning bush to go to the Israelites and save them from slavery. Moses asks the burning bush who he should say sent him, and God says through the burning bush, "I AM THAT I AM. Thus shalt thou say unto the children of Israel, I AM hath sent me unto you" (Exodus 3:14).

Dad taught me that the name of God is "I AM." Every time we utter those words, we are calling upon the name of God. When we say "I am," we are putting out to the universe what we are—meaning what we want—and we get back more of that. In this way, we create our own universe. Back to the Bible, there's a quote there that speaks to this idea: "Let the weak say, I am strong" (Joel 3:10). When we say, "I am weak," "I am sick," "I am not deserving of miracles," or "I am bad," we are blaspheming the name of God. Whenever we say, "I am," we are using the name of God that was given to us as a tool to create the life we want. So, as the Bible says, if you're sick, say, "I am strong." If you're poor, say, "I am abundant." We can change our lives just by changing what we say to ourselves.

∽

My dad loves to say, "If you have a choice to either be right or kind, choose kindness." I remember him demonstrating just that at a restaurant we go to frequently on Maui. Sands has always loved it, so we'd go there for him. However, none of us liked the waitress there, who seemed to make it her personal goal to say no to almost every request we had. For example, when I turned 13 I still wanted to order something from the "under 12" menu because I liked those portions better. Her answer was no, and her no was nonnegotiable. It got to the point that my instigating siblings and I would try to come up with requests that weren't on the menu just to see how many times she could tell us no in one meal.

Dad could have argued on our behalf—asked to see her manager, demanded she give us better service, or just stopped taking us there. But he was more interested in being kind than right. So one night he decided to make a change. "I am going to turn her around with kindness," he said. "I am going to make us her favorite customers and her our favorite waitress. Just watch."

The next time we went to this restaurant, Dad started off by asking the woman how her day was, where she was from, and if she had any family on the island. Then he gave her a genuine compliment on her new hairdo. When he asked for avocado on his salad this time around, she didn't object—she was happy to bring him the extra item, at no additional charge. Dad ended the meal with a generous tip, and told her we would come back again just to see her. Sure enough, when we went back a week or two later, she was all smiles when she saw us and even gave us a complimentary dessert. When I asked if I could order off the kids' menu, she winked at me and said, "No problem, baby." Not only did she like Dad all of a sudden, she liked me, too! Now when we go in there, she treats us like we're the Royal Family.

Dad made a decision to not be rude or "right" with her, because he felt that making her feel good was more important. He couldn't give away judgment or criticism, because he doesn't have those things inside of him. Instead, he honored the fact that both he and the waitress are part of God and looked at her as someone who needed an extra amount of love. Could he have argued against her and been right? Absolutely. But that wasn't important to him. What was important to him was giving away love and kindness, because he had extra of that to give.

To this day, if I encounter a surly waiter, barista, bartender, or flight attendant, I try to do what Dad modeled so well for me. I ask that person about their life, which is probably something that doesn't happen too often for people in the service industry. But honestly, a lot of the time I fail at this. If someone is rude to me, I want to be rude right back. If someone is snappy or has attitude, I want to be snappy and give attitude back to them. I would say that at this point in my life, I am at a 50 percent success rate when it comes to calming down and returning a terrible attitude with kindness. I am aware that what I'm doing is engaging in low-energy behavior, but I am still a work in progress.

Who Are You . . . Really?

My whole life I have heard people talk about the word *ego*. I was raised knowing what the ego was and that I had one—and that mine was big. As I grew up I learned to differentiate the work of the ego from the work of my highest self. I knew which one made me feel the best. Growing up, I had a huge desire to be right. (I'll be honest—I still do.) Not only that, if I was wrong and knew I was wrong, I was rarely nice about it. If someone bruised my ego, I would sometimes try to make them feel bad. I'd attempt to manipulate the conversation or debate so that I could come out on top. Knowing this about myself, I now try to admit right away when I am wrong, and to do so in a genuinely kind way. It ain't always easy!

One of my less enlightened habits is replaying conversations over and over in my mind, because my ego can't get over the fact that I was wrong. When I have a fight or argument with someone, I often still feel fired up about it hours after the fight has ended, and replay the conversation over and over. Sometimes I will be driving and wonder how in the heck I got wherever I ended up, because the whole time I'd been having a fight with someone in my head.

This is all the work of the ego. The ego says I need to be right, no matter what. If that means having an imaginary fight in my head after the fact, so be it. This is a habit I'm still working to break. I want to break it because I know that my highest self wants peace, and replaying conversations in my head pulls me away from that peace—no matter how good or "right" it makes me feel. Instead, the work of the highest self would be to stop the narrative and re-peat the mantra *I am peace I am,* or *I am love I am.* Maybe even go and meditate, to try to let go of the angst the ego is craving. Just like everyone else, I need to remember that inside, underneath the ego, we are all pieces of God.

Perpetuating imaginary fights is not the only thing the ego is good at. It also tells us that we are what we wear, what we have, what our accomplishments are, and what other people think of us. Many of us, myself included, have at times believed that these things do make us who we are. The ego says, "Forget about the little spark of God that's within you. What's important is winning, accomplishing things, and being the best." Our ego says we are what we do, so if we're not "doing," then we . . . aren't. We don't exist. If we believe we are what we have and then we lose what we have, we are nothing.

The stress and anxiety that come with trying to be the best are a waste. Someone will always come along and do it better than you. Applying stress might get your kids to work harder or get you more money, but it won't allow your perfect essence to come out. Your dharma will not be served. And besides, when this body goes we don't take money and grades with us. We take the evolution of our soul, and nothing more.

Being able to let things be—especially when it comes to your children or other family members—is what your highest self wants. (The Beatles had it right!) When you let things be, you allow God—the source, the individualized expression of that which you are—to come out and do what it is meant to do.

Look at the storms of your life, the really bad times. You will likely find that, after having gone through them, you were more compassionate and kind on the other side. If you are able to look at those storms and find the meaning and purpose within them, you may ultimately give thanks for them. I think of this quote by Elisabeth Kübler-Ross:

> The most beautiful people we have known are those who have known defeat, known suffering, known struggle, known loss, and have found their way out of the depths. These persons have an appreciation, a sensitivity, and an understanding of life that fills them with compassion, gentleness, and a deep loving concern. Beautiful people do not just happen.

Maya Angelou once wrote: "You may not control all the events that happen to you, but you can decide not to be reduced by them." This line comes to mind when I think of children who are being bullied, for instance. The experience of being bullied can change a person, but it doesn't have to make them smaller. Being bullied can make someone compassionate, forgiving, and authentic—qualities that bullies themselves might like to have. But because they don't carry these things around inside of them, they can't give them away. I would like to tell bullied kids to hang on; one day they might be able to look back on the pain they're in and be grateful for it.

It may seem impossible now, but one day, we really can look back at the storms we have weathered and give a silent thank you. For many of us, it is the storms of our lives that have given us compassion, kindness, and gentleness that we otherwise may not have known—and that we can now give away to others, because they are inside of us. As Mastin Kipp said, "When the universe takes something from your grasp, it is not punishing you, but merely opening your hands to receive something better."

An Eye for an Eye

In my family, gossip and negative talk weren't encouraged. We didn't sit around discussing what we disliked or who we disapproved of. My parents had no tolerance for us talking negatively about others. I realized that I'd never get their attention if I spoke unkindly about someone, so instead I began to look for kids in my class I did like—kids who were funny and did funny things—and I shared the stories about them with my family.

I also remember something that happened during a sleepover I had with my girlfriends. We were all lying in our sleeping bags in the living room, gossiping about another girl who wasn't there. The girl we were talking about was often mean to us and others, like a bully, which made it feel okay to talk negatively about her. I felt that she deserved it in some way because of her poor behavior.

Of course, Dad popped his head in the room right at that moment. (One thing about my father is that he has this uncanny way of showing up just when I know I am doing something wrong.) He looked me dead in the eye and scolded me, saying that he and my mom had raised me better than to talk about others like that.

I tried to justify the gossip session by explaining that this girl was the real bully, but he was having none of it. "If someone comes at you in a judgmental way and you judge them for it," he said, "you just doubled the amount of judgment in the space you're both in."

I remember trying to brush him off, saying something like, "Okay, cool, Dad, we all know you like peace and love and all that hippie stuff." But I wasn't getting off that easily. In truth I was totally ashamed, because I knew he was right. Even so, part of me wanted to be able to talk negatively about people like my other friends did, and not be made to feel so guilty! But such was not my fate. Before he left the room, Dad told all of us, "An eye for an eye makes the whole world blind. Don't forget that." I wanted to bury myself in my sleeping bag I was so embarrassed.

Now that I'm an adult myself, I'm always interested when I see acquaintances posting positive quotes and inspirational messages on Facebook and Twitter, yet I know that they're incredibly judgmental in their day-to-day lives. I hear them talk poorly about their friends and see them treat some people better than others. It's as if they don't believe the waitress is of the same caliber as the priest or lawyer, and therefore she does not deserve the same kind treatment. Now, please understand that I have been guilty of these same judgmental behaviors. We're all evolving. But I am becoming ever more aware of the judgment that creeps into my life. I observe it, even embrace it, and then let it go. I'm trying to live more positively, knowing that who I used to be, or what I used to do, does not shape who I am or what I do today.

I was taught that we become what we think about, like it or not. If we think in terms of judgment and criticism and competitiveness, we're going to attract more of the same into our lives.

We can *talk* about positivity until the cows come home. But if we have constant thoughts of negativity, we will only find more negativity showing up in our lives. In order to see things change, we have to change the way we think about things. As the Abraham-Hicks teachings say, stop telling it like it is and start telling it like you want it to be. Life isn't happening to you, it is *responding* to you. And the wonderful and inspirational Kris Carr says, "You can't please everyone. When you're too focused on living up to other people's standards, you aren't spending enough time raising your own. Some people may whisper, complain, and judge. But for the most part, it's all in your head. People care less about your actions than you think. Why? They have their own problems!"

Several years ago my dad had the opportunity to perform the marriage between Portia de Rossi and Ellen DeGeneres, which was extremely exciting. (In my eyes, it was one of the coolest things he has ever done!) Weeks later, someone asked him at one of his talks if he was "okay with that sort of thing"—meaning gay marriage. Dad later told me that at one point he would have given this person an earful about how we are all God's children, and it isn't our place to judge anyone for anything. But this time, he felt only love for the person who was so clearly *not* "okay with that sort of thing." Dad said that he realized it was his own growth that allowed him to bring light, rather than more darkness and condemnation. I can only hope I will eventually be able to bring the same in a consistent way because as I said, right now I am about 50/50.

Even though I sometimes felt embarrassed by my parents when I was a kid, and the lessons they instilled in me were sometimes painful, I could not be more grateful today. The lessons have stuck. I know that I can't give away what I don't have, so I place my attention on cultivating the things I *want* to be giving away—love, happiness, and understanding. And if you wonder whether that sleepover lecture stuck with me, the answer is yes. Recently I heard someone judging another person for being a bully. And what popped into my mind? *Oh, no way! Dad, we need to tell these people that an eye for an eye makes the whole world blind.*

WAYNE'S RESPONSE

The title of this chapter seems so obvious, and yet it is one of the most misunderstood of my ten secrets for success and inner peace. Of course you can't give away what you don't have, but the logic of this seems to disappear when it comes to the most esteemed thing a person can ever give away, and that is *love*. My message to all of my children was a recurring theme in our household: You must first love yourself and be filled with love in order to be able to give it away. Once you are filled with that love and it is all that you have inside of you, then that is all that you will have to give away.

The words offered in 1 John 4:16 have long been the guiding principle in my life as a student, teacher, and parent: "God is love, and who remains in love remains in God, and God remains in him." This is the essence behind all of the stories that Serena related in this chapter. *God is love.* What a sensational idea. God is not someone to fear—what is there to fear in pure, nonjudgmental love? This to me is our mission here on Earth, to become more like God. The means for arriving at this exalted place of Divine love is to practice having love and respect for yourself. This is the reason I would not tolerate having hateful and judgmental thoughts come out of my children, without challenging them to examine what they were keeping inside.

If you have only love inside and a surly waitress appears on your radar screen, that is precisely what you will have to give away. And by doing so, you will be an emissary of love. The highly revered spiritual teacher St. John of the Cross once observed, "Where there is no love, put love, and you will find love." By putting love in the presence of that impolite waitress, we were all able to see love do its magical work and convert anguish into love right on the spot.

I would frequently cite that passage from the New Testament and ask my children to interchange the words *God* and *love,* because we are told that God *is* love. I wanted Serena to know in her heart that in every moment that she was able to be in a feeling of love, she was literally acting as a host to God . . . that is, God is remaining in her in all moments of love.

The way to come to this realization is to practice, on a daily basis, giving love away. In the famous prayer of St. Francis, he asks, "Where there is hatred, let me bring love"—or, in interchanging the words *love* and *God,* "Where there is hatred, let me bring God."

This idea applies not only to love, but in all other areas of life as well. As I have said many times, "There is no way to happiness; happiness is the way." You must first have happiness lodged firmly within, and that is what you will bring to everything you do.

"What you keep inside you," I would tell my children, "is what you will have to give away. And once you truly understand and practice this idea, then it will become your own personal habit." I have persistently encouraged them to bring to all of their endeavors what they would most like to receive. Bring kindness to every encounter, regardless of whether they were the recipient of kindness; give away what they have inside and it would be returned to them. It's the Law of Attraction, and it never sleeps or even takes a temporary holiday. "You cannot find happiness by bringing unhappiness to your classes at school, or to your homework, or to your friendships," I'd tell them. "You must decide to be filled with joy, and this is what you will bring to every encounter—this is what you will give away. And guess what? This is what you will see returning to you as well. But if you bring your own sadness to what you think of as a sad or unhappy occasion, you will simply be doubling the amount of negativity, and then blaming the person or the nature of the event for your own discontent."

This lesson, once mastered, is a major key to a lifetime of success and inner peace.

CHAPTER 4

EMBRACE SILENCE

"Silence is the universal refuge, the sequel to all dull discourses and all foolish acts, a balm to our every chagrin, as welcome after satiety as after disappointment."

— HENRY DAVID THOREAU

I used to think that silence was something to avoid, and I'd go to great lengths to make sure it was never around me. Back when I was in college, for example, I remember turning on the TV, the radio, and the computer while I did my homework. All that noise somehow gave me comfort. Today, I rarely turn on the radio, even in my car. I've come to prefer the quiet. Not that it isn't challenging, thanks to cell phones, e-mails, text messages, Facebook alerts, Twitter . . . the list goes on and on. But I find silence to be my mind's refuge. Ever since I've begun to embrace it, I have become healthier, calmer, and more at peace with my life—to me, silence is heaven-sent!

My parents have always been comfortable in silence, and honestly, it used to really piss me off. When my dad would get in the car he would immediately turn the radio off, and I hated that (although now I do it, too!). But there is no one I know who embodies the idea of embracing silence more than my mom. When I was a kid, she was something of a mystery to me. In many ways, she still is. I sometimes wonder, are all mothers mysteries? Do they all keep their inner wisdom and knowing to themselves, or is mine the only one? You see, my mother is *quiet,* and that is one word that no one on the planet would ever use to describe me. So I was fascinated by her.

As a child, I viewed the loudest and most gregarious person in the room to be the best. I had no fear of public speaking and would gladly get up in front of my classroom—or the entire school, for that matter. Because of this, I was called on a lot, which I thought meant I was the best. Maybe not the absolute best in the whole class, but definitely one of them. I felt sorry for the kids who kept to themselves and seemed nervous when they spoke. I guess it's safe to say that I assumed quietness meant weakness. To that end, I thought Mom was the lesser of my parents, because she couldn't command the room the way Dad could. As a teen I also felt that I could out-talk, out-argue, and out-prove her any day. And she would always let me—she didn't want to argue and has never been good at it.

Mom didn't gossip with her friends, and I don't think I've ever heard her say she hated anything. When she drove my siblings and me to school or an appointment, she often became involved in our conversations, but she also wasn't afraid to just sit back and listen. She never gave attention to our fights, which meant there was no audience to fight in front of. Because of this there was no "winning," and our arguments almost always stopped immediately.

Since I have been writing this book, I have been reflecting on my life—especially my childhood. I remember so many Sunday dinners when my whole family would be sitting around the table. There would be as many as 12 adults (including my older siblings and their significant others, my parents and grandparents, and even some friends) and tons of kids, and my mom would have made a beautiful meal for everyone to enjoy. She never once piped up to ask how it tasted or looked defeated if her work went unacknowledged.

My mother is not the type who needs praise or attention, and she doesn't tend to command an audience. But of course, when she uses it, her voice always has the biggest impact in the house. I have learned so much about how effective staying quiet can be from her.

An Ocean of Calm

Mom has always been very involved in the lives of all of her children. Each of us still calls her every morning, dumping our worries and problems and triumphs and failures into her lap. We get off the phone feeling better about ourselves, and all she did was listen.

As a child I felt she was somehow distant from me because she didn't tell me everything she was thinking. Now I understand that she was exhibiting her greatest gift. She was demonstrating that by being quiet, you allow your body and mind to heal. Even though Dad has written about the topic of embracing silence, it always brings up thoughts of Mom. She showed us every day, in her quiet way, that it is not torture or punishment, and it is not a sign of weakness or lack of intelligence. Embracing silence is wise. It requires strength and discipline. It forces us to look at ourselves, so we can make better choices. As Blaise Pascal observed, "All man's miseries derive from not being able to sit quietly in a room alone." That's something my mom has always known how to do.

This reminds me of something that happened when I was in high school. The day after I got my wisdom teeth removed, I went to a friend's house to hang out. To my chagrin, opening my mouth was so painful that every time I tried to talk I had to stop immediately. Eventually I realized that all I could do was sit and listen. At first it made me want to leave, but then my friend started to open up about a problem she was having with her boyfriend. I just listened to her talk, nodding my head so she knew I was following along.

As I was getting ready to leave, I remember her telling me the strangest thing. "Thank you so much," she said. "Your advice really helped me. Now I know what I need to do."

I smiled and mouthed that she was welcome, but left feeling baffled. I hadn't given her any advice—I had hardly said anything at all! Yet the result was that she felt I had helped her figure out a difficult situation.

As I drove home that day I realized that's what Mom had been doing for all of us our entire lives. She was an ocean of calm who easily alleviated our stress and worry. She didn't pry; she didn't try to get information out of us; and she didn't gossip with us. She merely sat there and listened. Listening to someone—really *hearing* them—is one of the greatest gifts we can give. It took me years to recognize what my mother had been demonstrating all along. I think that's the funny part. She never *told* me to listen; she never said to embrace silence. That would have been counter to what she was teaching. She simply lived it.

When people meet my mother, they typically remark how mellow and peaceful she is given that she is the mother of seven children and stepmother to one more! When people ask her how she does it, she tells them it's because she has been meditating regularly since she was 12 years old.

As long as I can remember, Mom has had a sign that says Mom IS MEDITATING, which goes on her door twice a day. My siblings and I have always known that when she was meditating, she was in silence and shouldn't be disturbed unless it was really important. There was a time when she had children aged 1, 3, 5, 7, 9, 15, and 16, and could have easily come up with the excuse not to continue her meditation practice. But she continued to take that time for herself, and as children we all honored it.

Having her disappear for half an hour twice a day also meant we got to learn how to take care of ourselves. The older kids would help out with the younger ones, so that Mom could really have peace. We would *never* have knocked on her door when her little sign was up. Not out of fear of her response, but out of fear of what our brothers and sisters would say! It was a cardinal rule in the house. Everyone knew Mom needed that time.

My sister Sommer has always been the wildest in the family. She's 21 months older than I am, and as a kid I idolized her. Sommer is the type of person who does not have a problem breaking the rules. I can remember one time when we were flying to Maui and she made it her personal goal not to wear the seat belt the whole way there without getting caught. It was the most exciting

12 hours I have ever spent on a plane because the rest of us kids were scanning the aisle every five minutes to see if the flight attendant was coming by and Sommer would get in trouble (which she never did.)

Anyway, one time when Mom went in to meditate, Sommer calmly walked into the garage and got her Rollerblades on—then came back in and started skating around the living room and kitchen. We were not supposed to skate in the house, and I told her she was going to get caught. She looked at me like I was so dumb and said, "I set the timer for 25 minutes. Mom never comes out before 30 minutes, so get your Rollerblades on. Time is running out."

I scrambled to get mine on, and she and I started chasing each other through the living room and kitchen as fast as we could. At one point we ended up colliding and knocking over a floor lamp that fell on its side and got a huge crack in it. Sommer immediately raced to get her Rollerblades off and ran upstairs to get Saje, who was about four at the time. Sommer told me to get my skates off and turn off the timer, while she coolly explained to our sister that if she wanted to play with us the next time we had friends over, she needed to lie down while we placed the broken lamp on top of her, and pretend to be hurt when our mom came out.

Saje, who always wanted to play with the older kids, happily agreed to go along with Sommer's plan. She lay down, and we gently placed the broken lamp on top of her. When we heard Mom's bedroom door open, we gave Saje the signal so she could start pretend crying. Sommer and I clamored all over ourselves to tell our mother how we had no idea how this had happened—Saje probably bumped into it being clumsy. Mom replied that she was just happy Saje was okay and wasn't worried about the lamp.

Saje was the worst fake crier I have ever seen, and to this day I don't know how we didn't get caught, but thank God for Mom's dedication to meditation. For the next few weeks, Sommer and I got our Rollerblades on the second our mother's bedroom door closed and had 25 minutes of pure bliss—just using a little more caution around the lamps.

Meditation and the Subconscious Mind

When I was five years old, Mom and Dad took my siblings and me to our friend Katrina's house in the mountains of Maui. Katrina was going to teach us kids Transcendental Meditation. Each of us was to be given a special mantra, so we had to go into her house one at a time.

While waiting my turn, I decided to be the comedian and tease the cows in Katrina's pasture. I went up to a rather large bull and started to fake sneeze at it. Each time I did, the bull would turn and look at me—which was making my brothers and sisters laugh. On my third sneeze, the bull charged at me, head first. I ran as fast as my little legs could carry me, ducking under a fence just in time to get out of the bull's path. After that I ran back to the car and refused to get out. I sat there with Mom, Dad, and Sands, who was only three years old at the time, while everyone else played outside. Mom and Dad decided to meditate while we waited. Of course my siblings and I knew that when our parents meditated we had to be quiet. We never questioned that or bothered them during their meditation—until this particular day.

Sands was very worried that the cows, or the "woowas," as he called them, would get in the car. He asked repeatedly—I mean at least 100 times—if the woowas would get in. My parents were both in their meditative state, so neither of them replied. Over and over, Sands asked, "Dad, will the woowas get in the car?" Finally, Mom opened her eyes, looked at Dad, and said, "Wayne, answer him." With his eyes still closed, Dad replied. "No, Sands, the woowas won't get in the car." Then my parents both went right back to meditating.

I remember looking at Sands and thinking what an idiot he was and that *of course* the woowas would not get in the car. Nonetheless, I was happy to hear the definitive answer from Dad. (After my scare with the bull, I needed a little extra confirmation.) The point of this story is that my parents didn't get mad at Sands for asking the same question over and over while they were meditating. They didn't yell at him or tell him to shut up. In fact, they never did those things to any of us. I think because they meditated so frequently, they were both naturally calm. Raising their voices with their children was something they just didn't do.

Eventually Sommer came out of Katrina's house and told me it was my turn to go in and learn my mantra. I was irritated that she'd gotten to go first and already had her fancy mantra word. I was determined to go in there and be the best at whatever this meditation thing was. I think that if God ever had a laugh, He probably got a good one at a five-year-old wanting to be "the best" meditator.

I walked into Katrina's house and sat in her meditation room while she explained that she was indeed going to give me a word, which would become my mantra. Then she said that I would sit in silence and repeat the word over and over in my mind, until eventually my mind became unattached from my thoughts and I could experience complete and utter silence. I was stunned. So *that's* what this Transcendental Meditation thing was all about? Another one of my parents' weird tricks to try to get me to be quiet? It sounded like a nightmare, but I couldn't exactly get up and walk out.

I tried to keep my eyes closed as she chanted my mantra over and over again. The word I was given to repeat as my mantra was *inga.* I'm not sure what it means or why I was given that word—all I remember was peeking out frequently, hoping to catch a glimpse of her cat and invite it to come over. I figured this weirdo (I mean that lovingly) had her eyes shut, so I wouldn't get caught.

When the training was finally over, Katrina told me that using my mantra would help me quiet my mind and stay in a constant state of conversation with God. But, she said, it would take a lot of practice. Looking back, I see that as the understatement of the century—especially for the five-year-old me. Dad used to tell me, "Serena, you have two ears and one mouth for a reason. You need to talk less and listen more." He actually used to call me "Mouth," because I never shut up.

It's taken me more than 20 years to use the powerful gift of meditation that my parents gave me. But now when I practice it,

I sink in so deep that I often finish the meditation and realize that I haven't had a thought in 40 minutes! My "monkey mind" stops swinging from thought to thought and fear to fear and desire to desire; it actually takes a break. When I come out of a meditation I feel foggy for a few minutes, and I have to drink a lot of water to feel normal again. It's as if my body is so disoriented from the silence that it gets confused—like, where the heck are we and what just happened?! The funny thing is, I don't technically meditate in silence; I use a meditation CD called *The I AM Wishes Fulfilled Meditation*, which my dad put out a few years ago. But there is an inner silence that takes hold.

By meditating, I am slowly reprogramming myself to believe that I am a person who is capable of silence. I've stopped telling myself that being silent is harder for me than for others, or that it's not my fault that I talk so much, or that I really can't change. Instead, when these thoughts creep in, I just observe them and let them go out the same way they came.

I'm happy to report that I've gotten better at embracing silence over the years. (But only a little.) If you struggle with this concept like I do, try just turning the car radio off when you're going for a quick drive. Or even better, turn the TV off for the last five minutes before you go to sleep and silently thank God for everything you have in your life. One of my favorite sayings goes something like, "If the only prayer you ever say is 'thank you,' that will be enough."

Observing our thoughts and embracing silence is especially important before we fall asleep. As my dad teaches, whatever you're thinking about in the last five minutes before you fall asleep—that is, before your subconscious mind takes over—that's what you will marinate in for the next eight hours. So if you spend that time running through all the struggles of your day, you're programming yourself with those negative thoughts.

You see, the subconscious can't differentiate between what you're "really" experiencing and what you're thinking. It acts in alignment with the energy you're putting out into the world. This is why you get what you think about—like it or not. So when you program in what you *didn't* like about your day, you are un-wittingly telling your subconscious that you want *more* of that. Understanding this, I do my best to consciously shift into positive thinking before I go to bed. I turn off the TV and spend some time thinking about the things that give me joy and peace before I go to sleep.

When we are quiet and focus on our thoughts, we're able to re-alize what kind of thinking patterns we have, and change the ones that aren't working for us anymore. I was always taught that if I changed the way I was thinking, and began to cancel out thoughts that didn't serve me and replace them with thoughts that did, my entire life would begin to look more how I wanted it to. And I can say conclusively that this has worked for me.

God's One and Only Voice

I went to a Christian school as a kid, and I remember my friends thinking that you could only talk to God when you had your hands folded in church. I tried to tell a boy in my class that I talked to God all the time, and he said I was lying. I was very upset and told my parents about this, and they said that I should try to teach my classmate that God was everywhere and could be talked to by anyone at any time. It was then I began to understand that I was "different," and so were my parents. They encouraged me to ask questions and find my own truth, rather than blindly adhere to what was written down in a book, what I was taught, or what the current fad was. I realized that the only way to find those inner truths was to go within, and that meant turning down the sound in my head.

Many times when I'd visit friends, I'd hear loud talking, yell-ing, and even fighting in their households. I never saw this be-tween my parents. I'm sure Mom and Dad had arguments, but not in front of us as children. Growing up, I discovered that when I was around peaceful people, I tended to feel more peaceful myself. When I was around noisy, volatile people, I'd get anxious and not feel very good. The same goes for what was happening in my own mind. When the volume was turned way up in my head, I tended to get stressed out. When my mind was quiet, and I allowed my thoughts to come and go, I felt calm.

When I was a kid, one of the best ways for me to turn the sound down was to go outside, and it's still that way for me. I recognize God in nature more than in a church, temple, or place of worship. I feel that all of God's glory can be seen when we're outside, rather than in the confinement of four walls. Whenever my family and I took trips to the beach or to the mountains, I'd feel an overwhelming sense of peace and fun. I'd always felt that it was okay to be myself—in church, I didn't feel that. I was aware that I was singing songs and repeating words that someone else had written; they weren't my own. Don't get me wrong, I understand that church is the best place for some people to feel close to God and to enjoy the silence. It's just not been the case for me.

Mother Teresa once said, "God is the friend of silence. See how nature—trees, flowers, grass—grow in silence; see the stars, the moon and sun, how they move in silence. . . . We need silence to be able to touch souls."

Just this year I realized that I have tons and tons of thoughts a day that don't really serve me. Sometimes I catch myself in long, anxiety-filled conversations in my mind or, as I said before, replays of arguments I've had. This kind of thinking only serves to make me feel more anxious. When I catch myself, I stop these thoughts immediately and begin focusing on the good—on what I like, what's going well for me, and other positive things.

Where we find ourselves in life is the product of all of our thoughts. If we don't like where we are, then we must change our way of thinking. Thoughts are energy, and we get what we think about. When we do whatever we find to be an effective way to turn down life's volume, it's much easier to become an observer of our thoughts. We then have the space to ask ourselves whether the thoughts going through our heads really serve us—or whether quieting the mind might get us closer to where we want to go. As Herman Melville once wrote, "God's one and only voice is silence." When we embrace silence, we allow God—our intuition, our inner calling, whatever we want to call it —to speak up, loud and clear.

Mom's Miracle

My mother learned her most important lesson about silence when she was alone and in labor with my oldest brother, Shane. It happened four decades ago, but she's never forgotten it. It's a story I've heard over and over, and it still leaves me in a state of wonder. I asked her if she'd tell her story here, in her own words, and she agreed. I am grateful to be able to share it with you, and feel it's the perfect way to end this chapter:

> I was 23 and pregnant with my first child. I went back home to Pennsylvania to give birth so I could be near my mother. I was due on April 14, 1974. When I got to Pennsylvania, I found a new obstetrician. When I saw him on the 22nd of March, which was a Friday, he told me there were no changes in the baby's position. He said my child would come close to my due date. But that Sunday night, my water broke. At 1:20 A.M., I called down to my parents, and they took me to the hospital. Because my water had broken, they admitted me to stay even though I was still in the very early stages of labor. I had not had a single contraction, so I had a long way to go. My mother decided to stay, and my father went home. In those days family stayed in the visitors' room, so I was all alone.
>
> At 2 A.M., I had the most intense and excruciating contraction. I remember thinking, *Oh my Lord, how am I going to do this?* I had planned on having a drug-free birth, but that first contraction had me doubt whether I could do it.
>
> Right after my contraction a nurse came in and asked if I was okay. I told her I wasn't sure if I could do this, and that I was praying for help. The nurse took one of my hands in hers. With her other hand, she smoothed

my hair back and ran her palm across my forehead very gently. Looking into my eyes, she said, "There is a place within you to breathe. Go there now, and you will not suffer." I closed my eyes and focused on my breathing as she left. A little more than two hours later, I awoke with a great urge to push.

They had a call button to contact the nurse, so I squeezed it. Eventually a different nurse came in and said, "Oh, you woke up." I thought this was weird, because I didn't know I had been sleeping. I told her I was pretty sure my child was ready to come out now. The nurse sort of laughed and said, "You haven't even begun labor, honey, you're not ready to push. You probably just have to go to the bathroom." I told her that I knew I was a first-time mom and didn't have experience, but that I was pretty sure I was ready to push. I begged her to check my dilation. To placate me, she checked—and she looked completely shocked.

She told me that my baby's head was right there. That I had been correct—I needed to push. She then admitted she hadn't even phoned my obstetrician yet, so I would have to use the doctor on call. She quickly wheeled me into the delivery room. They didn't even have me move onto the delivery bed because I was completely ready to go. The doctor on call at the hospital came into the room and told me that with my next contraction I would need to push.

I waited and waited, but no contraction came. He asked me why I hadn't started pushing, and I said that I was waiting for my next contraction. But no contractions came! I told him the only contraction I'd felt had been over two hours ago.

The doctor looked at the two nurses and said, "What did you give her?"

They replied, "We didn't give her anything! She slept through her entire labor."

I was hearing all of this but wasn't paying much attention because I was so focused on the desire to push. I asked the doctor if I could start pushing without the contraction and he said, "Yes, yes! Push!" Seven or eight pushes later, my son Shane was born.

Later that day I walked over to the nursery to see my baby. A nurse walked up to me and said, "So you're the one everyone is talking about!" I was embarrassed, so I just smiled at her. She said everyone was talking about me because I'd had a pain-free delivery.

I felt awkward, as if I had to defend my labor. So I said, "Well, I did have one contraction."

She asked, "How did you do it?"

"Well," I said to her, "if it wasn't for that nurse who helped me, I don't know how I would have done it." She looked surprised and asked me which nurse had been of such help to me. I told her that I didn't know her name, but she had red hair and had been wearing a blue dress, and she had a real softness to her. I told her that she'd told me there was a place in me to breathe, and to go there and I wouldn't suffer.

The nurse stood there staring at me. Eventually she said, "I have worked in labor and delivery for 13 years, and we don't have anyone here who fits that description. We also have never worn blue." The nurse said that she didn't know what I had experienced, but it certainly had been a gift.

At the time, I was too young and immature to grasp that gift or have an understanding of it. As I went on to go through birth and labor six more times, I ultimately felt the depth of that moment. I haven't since had a birth quite like I did with my son Shane, but I was able to use breathing and meditation to bring each of my children into the world in a way that was peaceful for both of us. I am still growing into an understanding of the experience today.

What I learned that night was that I could go through birth and labor without drugs. I also learned that birth required me to go deep within myself to find the strength there. During my subsequent labors, I embraced silence. I didn't talk to anyone while I was in labor, and I went into the pain without fear. I don't feel special or Divine or more gifted than anyone else. I believe I received this gift because I asked for it, and because I believed it was possible.

Since the birth of my brother Shane, my mother has given birth to the rest of us without any pain medication, while in complete silence. If there is anything she has taught me, it is that in silence, we allow God to enter.

I used to perceive silence as weakness, but now I understand. Silence is strength. Silence is wisdom. Silence is God. Thank you, Mom, so much, for teaching me this lesson through your own silent grace.

WAYNE'S RESPONSE

I have long known the wisdom inherent in the ancient aphorism, "It's the silence between the notes that makes the music." This is a truth that both Marcelene and I attempted to convey to all of our children as we sought to make our home a temple of serenity and peace, amidst all of the activity of a large family. Everything emerges out of the silence. There could be no music without the silence; it would be just one long note without the interruptions. Meditation is the only way I know for merging into those interruptions and while there, making conscious contact with the source of all creation.

I have been on a regimen of daily meditation for over three continuous decades, and I personally know the tremendous benefits that accrue with a regular practice. Most of the significant quantum changes that took place in my life were the result of sudden flashes of insight that came from quieting my mind and listening, by shutting down the incessant inner dialogue and staying in conscious contact with God. In all the years of my lecturing and writing I have used meditation as my guidepost for what to say onstage, or at my own sacred writing space. This is the time when I listen and ask and then get very quiet. It is a place of pure inner peace and serenity.

Both Marcie and I introduced all of our children to this activity when they were very young. When the sign was on the door that Mom was meditating, the children were firmly reminded that this was a sacred time and was to be respected, just as if they were in a place of worship. All of Serena's stories in this chapter reflect the desire on the part of both of her parents to bring this amazing discipline to their lives.

I recall being at the cell on Robben Island off the coast of Cape Town, South Africa, where the legendary Nelson Mandela spent so many years in isolation and deep silence. In those many years as a prisoner, he would go within and listen attentively in profound silence. When he emerged from that incarceration, rather than being filled with anger, rage, and revenge, he instead had forgiveness and reconciliation as his uppermost priorities, and was able to avoid what many thought would become a rampage of killing and war.

I once heard the Dalai Lama say that if we could take every single child on planet Earth and have them meditate for one hour a week on compassion, we could eliminate all of the world's violence in one generation. This was the message Marcie and I wanted our children to not only hear as a lecture from us, but to see in action. As Lao-tzu observed in the Tao Te Ching, "Silence is a source of great strength." For me this is an absolute truism, and it was my mission to bring this truth not only to my children, but to the world as well. I have written an entire book (*Getting in the Gap*) on this subject of meditation, and produced four CDs using several different methods of meditation that have been helpful to me on this journey.

We live in a very loud world. Children today are exposed to a cacophony of inescapable noise, from radios and television to small-screen devices with headphones carrying endless sounds to their overworked ears. Sirens and construction noises, along with interminable voices that are bombarding them in almost all of their waking hours, keep them away from the silence. Serena included a quotation from Herman Melville, which she has heard me say hundreds of times throughout her lifetime: "God's one and only voice is silence." This is such a profound truth. It is from out of the indivisible silence that creation flows, and this is where we can all make direct contact with our source of being.

All of Serena's vignettes in this chapter reflect a message that originated with me in a very famous quotation from the Czech writer and poet Franz Kafka. I've had this reproduced and laminated, and it not only inspired me to write about and explore meditation, it also provoked my wife and me to raise our children in an atmosphere where silence and listening were emphasized over clamor and pandemonium:

> You need not do anything. Remain sitting at your table and listen. You need not even listen, just wait. You need not even wait, just learn to be quiet, still, and solitary. And the world will freely offer itself to you unmasked. It has no choice, it will roll in ecstasy at your feet.

I wanted all of our children to experience that ecstasy. It is what nature provides for us and is reflected in this contemplative poem offered by one of my all-time favorite scholars, Johann Wolfgang von Goethe (translation by Robert Bly):

> *Over all the hilltops*
> *Silence,*
> *Among all the treetops*
> *You feel hardly*
> *A breath moving.*
> *The birds fall silent in the woods.*
> *Simply wait! Soon*
> *You too will be silent.*

CHAPTER 5

GIVE UP YOUR PERSONAL HISTORY

"Don't look back, you're not going that way."
— ANONYMOUS

Several years ago, my parents separated. For their own reasons, they didn't want to officially go through with a divorce, but they live in different places, have their own houses, and date other people. As long as they're happy, safe, and healthy, I don't really get involved in what either of them do or who they're with. They've never meddled in my relationships, so it has never even occurred to me to meddle in theirs.

I don't view myself as coming from a "broken home"; as a result, I don't view my family as broken either. I made the choice not to let my parents' separation affect my relationships with my family members, and therefore it hasn't. Of course it was a big shock for all of us when Mom and Dad decided to split up, but they decided to do things differently—rather than retreating to their separate corners, they wanted us to remain a family in every sense. So we have Thanksgiving together every year, and we take a trip every summer as well.

A lot of people can't seem to understand that my parents separated in their own way and on their own terms, and some are appalled when they find out that Mom and Dad are still married and will most likely never get divorced. It's as if these people would themselves be more comfortable if my parents' relationship fit into a neat little box labeled either "married" or "divorced."

My mom and dad are still very good friends who get along well. When people ask how I can be so laid back about them separating, I tell them it's because I always knew it wasn't about me. My parents separated because it was what they needed to do. I wouldn't have wanted them to stay together if that wasn't what was best for each of them. I want them to be happy. If they're happier together, great. If they're happier separated, then great as well.

As Robert Frost said, "We love the things we love for what they are." I love my parents for who they are, together or apart. They are incredible people. I love who they are, not what their relationship looks like. I've chosen to give up my personal history around this one, and be present with all the new love and joy that are available today.

Changing and Growing as a Family

While my parents' separation has evolved into something that is nice, loving, and supportive, it didn't start off that way. It was a really difficult time for the whole family, yet I also think it was a pivotal time in my life. Who I was as a person changed dramatically, and since then I have never been quite the same as I was before. I don't think that's such a bad thing, though. Basically, my parents' separation forced me to grow up and put into practice some of the principles I had been raised on—including letting go of my personal history.

Mom and Dad announced their separation a few weeks before my 16th birthday. It came as a huge surprise for me and my siblings and basically everyone who knew us. If I were a betting woman, I would have put my money on the cards that said my parents would be together forever.

We have always spent every summer on Maui as a family and as we got older, we would fly out at different times depending on each of our school or work schedule. At this point, my dad was already in Maui, and my mom told me that I needed to fly out with Sands, Saje, and my best friend, Lauren; then she'd meet us there in two weeks. Although she and Dad had announced their decision to separate in early May, it seemed that they were working on whatever issue was driving them apart and the divorce topic was going to be put to rest. But then, after the two weeks had gone by, Mom decided not to come at all. That's when I realized that whatever was happening between them was serious and wasn't going away. Inside, I was devastated; on the outside, I put on a brave face.

My dad was distraught and had a very difficult time just functioning on a day-to-day basis during that fateful summer. He had always been so strong and positive that his pain was jarring. He was such a powerful figure in my mind, but that summer I realized he was also vulnerable and human. I understood that some pain has to be endured, and that all the books in the world won't take away the hurt that a broken heart can cause. I know that my mom was suffering, too, but I wasn't with her that summer and only spoke to her a few times, so I don't know exactly what she was going through. All I know is that she, like all of us, was miserable.

I was very angry and profoundly confused. I didn't understand why my parents couldn't work it out; I wanted them to get back together because the idea of them being apart was too hard to stomach. Yet in the immediate sense, I had to learn to serve my younger brother and sister first. They were 13 and 11 at the time, and their pain became more of a concern for me than what I was feeling inside. I kept it together and tried to remain strong, until the day that I still consider to be the hardest of my life.

Dad had taken Lauren, Sands, Saje, and me on a snorkeling trip to a little island called Molokini. On our way back, Mom called Dad, which was significant because they hadn't spoken for a few weeks. (They'd agreed to have some time apart and work on their issues separately.) Dad pulled over to the side of the road so they could talk, and the rest of us decided to get out and play along the beach while he was on the phone.

Sands was skipping these big, flat rocks along the water, and Saje walked in front of one of them, which cracked her hard in the side of her head. I heard a sickening pop as the rock hit her that I will never forget. A fountain of blood squirted out of her head and went straight up into the air, coming down all over her face and her body. I picked my sister up and began running down the beach, holding her as best as I could, and screamed for our dad. He turned around, saw Saje covered in blood, and dropped the phone. As he put her in the car so we could drive into town, I picked up the phone and heard my panicked mother shouting, "What happened to Saje? What happened to my baby?"

I was so angry at her for not being there. She would have known what to do in that instant, and would have made the whole thing better. I felt that she didn't even deserve an answer as to what was going on. I remember starting to say something like, "You should be here, you should be here with us!" Instead, I hung up on her and dialed 911.

The ambulance met us in a grocery-store parking lot, and the paramedics looked at Saje's head and said it wasn't that bad. The wound would need to be washed out thoroughly with soap and water, and then she'd be fine with a butterfly bandage. When we got home, I helped my sister into the shower and began washing her head. Almost immediately my finger went about an inch into her head, and I could see bone.

Separating her hair back from the cut, I realized that her wound was about twice as big and deep as we had originally thought. Once I pulled the hair back, she began to bleed a lot. I got her out of the shower and called our neighbor, who drove us down to the doctor. Dad had left to go pick up a pizza for dinner, thinking Saje was fine as the paramedics had said.

As our neighbor drove us, my sister held my hand and begged me not to let the doctor shave her head in case she needed stitches. She seemed so small to me, so vulnerable there without our parents. I would have done anything in the world to make her feel better in that moment, so I promised her I wouldn't let them shave any part of her head. Right after we arrived at the doctor's office, Dad came in, and the doctor announced that he needed to put staples and stitches on both the inner and outer part of her wound.

He said that he'd have to shave about five inches of her hair in order to make a clean incision, and Saje immediately began to sob.

I explained to the doctor that he couldn't do that because she needed all of her hair, and when he didn't seem to care, I lost it. I rapidly told him about the promise I had made her. I told him our parents were getting divorced, and keeping my word to my sister was really important because she needed to know she could count on me. I told him that if he shaved her head he would be hurting both of us. The doctor made me get out of the room and had a nurse hold her down while he shaved a part of her head. She lay there screaming, "Serena, you promised!" over and over again.

Looking back, I know it wasn't the broken promise or even Saje's head being shaved that had hurt us both so much. We were so destroyed emotionally in that instant because we needed our parents to be there to make things better, as they always had before—and for the first time in our lives, they weren't. Although Dad was there physically, emotionally and mentally he was somewhere else.

As I sat outside of that room and listened to my little sister scream my name to help her, all the while being unable to do anything, I had an epiphany. I needed our parents as much as Saje did, and I wasn't ready to shoulder the responsibility of making sure things were all right for my younger siblings or myself. For the first time, I discovered that the people you love can really let you down—but you still have to get up and move forward in spite of it. I wasn't ready to have to grow up and take charge, but that's exactly what I did.

I could see that my dad wasn't going to be able to handle anything that summer, and I wanted desperately to protect my younger brother and sister from seeing any of the things I was seeing. I put on an air of responsibility and maturity, and made it my job to ensure that everyone else was okay. Truth is, that was the most healing and helpful thing I could have done.

Saje and I weren't close before that summer, but after going through what we did, I felt a closeness with her that I still feel to this day. I have the same feeling toward Sands, too. I feel like we weathered something that was tough, and we did it togeth-er. I wouldn't change it for the world. (For various reasons, my older siblings weren't on Maui for most of that summer, so it really was just Sands, Saje, Lauren, and me all riding it out together.) The events of that summer definitely changed me, but I feel they changed me for the better. I became more of who I really am. I was not just my parents' child anymore—I was Serena. I look back at all of the events of that summer, and I feel grateful for them, hard times included.

Time really does heal all wounds. At the beginning of their separation, my parents couldn't really be around each other. But after about a year or so of confusion, hurt, and revenge-seeking behavior, they decided that enough was enough. They made the decision that the separation wasn't going to be bad for them or any of us. As a result, it really hasn't been. There have been lit-tle issues here and there, of course, but overall we are still a very close-knit family. I believe we always will be.

Other positive things came out of this as well: Dad eventually emerged from his dark cloud to write *The Power of Intention*, argu-ably his most influential work of the last 15 years. I also notice that I have a different kind of relationship with him now that he and Mom are separated—for reasons I can't really explain, we are much closer than we were. As for my mom, she went on to meet and fall in love with a man named Tony, who has become a part of our family. My parents now speak on the phone every day, and when Dad comes into town, he stays at Mom's house with her and Tony! My parents have a spiritual partnership, which, in my opin-ion, is the best kind of relationship you can have with anyone.

I could look at my family's situation and find reasons to be sad, but I don't. I choose to find the good in it. Even before their separation, Mom and Dad taught me that if you decide something is going to be bad—because that's what everyone, including your-self, assumes it will be—then it definitely *will* be bad. However, if you decide something as big as separating from your spouse is going to be easy and pain-free, then it will be.

Some people may read this and say, "Well, *I* want it to be pain-free, but there's no way he/she will let it be that way." The truth is, only we can control how we feel—because it's up to us how we choose to react to others' behavior. As my dad always says, how people treat you is their karma, how you react is yours. My parents didn't demonstrate this in the beginning, but for the last ten or so years, they've certainly made up for it!

Let Go and Live in the Now

Another reason I have chosen not to view my parents' separation as a problem is that I never wanted to label myself based on my personal history. Dad always says, "When you label me, you negate me." When we're given a label, there's often pressure to stay that way; to fit ourselves into that label. I've been taught that just because I have always done something the same way, that doesn't mean I have to continue doing it that way. My history does not have to define me. Instead, I've been encouraged to try new things, to be adventurous, and not to be afraid to fail.

Our personal history is all the things in our background that keep us the same. If more of the same is not what we want, we have to let go of our history. When we do, we let go of all the beliefs we've had about ourselves—beliefs which may not even be true. Perhaps you came from a divorced family, and you've taken on the belief that it has really held you back in life. Take it from me, you can choose to view that situation differently. In letting go of the past, you may find that you're able to be more alive in the present. If you don't like where you are in life, then you *must* change your way of thinking. As my friend, the poet Nancy Levin, says, "Each day—let go. Everything is at stake."

How many times a day do you catch yourself contemplating the past—analyzing it or agonizing over it? I know I spend more time doing that than I would like. When I become present, on the other hand, I let go of the stress and anxiety that come with living in the past. For me, letting go of my personal history has been a key step toward living in the moment.

I have met so many people who believe that they cannot live the life they want to live because of past events, and they just feel stuck. To be honest with you, that sort of scares me. I would never want to live in a universe where I felt I wasn't in control of how I respond.

I understand that not everyone is born into the same type of family that I was, so not everyone feels empowered enough to believe that they can create the life they want. I would argue, however, that everyone has a voice inside of them—a sense that there is a force greater than themselves operating in the universe. That greater thing, which I call God, would never be discouraging; it patiently listens and waits for each of us.

I have often had a hard time understanding why bad things happen to people who are positive and living a life on purpose. How is it that tragic things happen to people who aren't doing bad things? Then I heard Dad say something that really clicked with me. He said that Abraham (a collection of entities channeled by Esther Hicks) explained that when bad things happen, it isn't because we deserved it. It is not punishment for some past life or karmic debt. Bad things happen because we are aligned with them. Why we are aligned with negativity doesn't matter. But if we can accept that we were somehow aligned with it, we can move past it. We can take responsibility for it, let it go, and start living in the present moment. Living in the now allows us to generate the energy that will take us wherever we want to go in life.

Taking responsibility for something doesn't mean that it is our fault; instead, it means that we are no longer going to allow someone else's actions to have an impact on how we feel or operate in our lives. Taking responsibility for it means taking the reins of our own life. As Eckhart Tolle has said, "Stay fully present in the now—your whole life unfolds here. In the now there is joy of being and deep peace."

Making Peace with the Past

We all know people who have suffered enormous hardships and tremendous loss. I happen to be best friends with someone who has had to endure more pain in a few years than many people do in a lifetime.

Lauren's father passed away in an accidental fire when she was 19. A short time later, as all of her friends were going off to college, she decided to stay back and live at home in order to help her mom, Lorraine, who was really ill with cancer. Soon Lauren became her mother's primary caregiver, as Lorraine's condition worsened.

When Lauren and I would talk on the phone, I'd tell her about who was hooking up with who and what kind of parties were going on. Meanwhile, she'd tell me what chemo and radiation were really like. Her attitude, however, was positive the entire time. Although we talked about how heartbroken she was at watching her mother become more and more sick, I never heard an ounce of self-pity from her.

Lauren and her mom were even able to keep up their amazing sense of humor throughout Lorraine's entire illness. I remember once Lauren told me how the other patients didn't appreciate her mom listening to songs like "Disco Inferno" and "Rock and Roll, Hoochie Koo" while they were going through something as serious as chemotherapy. Lauren and Lorraine, however, were able to find a way to laugh together even in the darkest of times.

While all of Lauren's friends, myself included, were partying and living up the college life, she was serving her mother in the most profound way possible. Lauren would feed her, bathe her, and make her laugh. She would play music for her and cook for her and make sure she was always comfortable in her last months of life. Shortly before Lorraine passed away, she made us promise that we would go to Italy and make a toast to her over some amazing food and wine. Lorraine's attitude was so uplifting even while she knew she was dying.

In the same week that I received my diploma, Lauren buried her mom. She spent years in the highest form of service, never asking what was in it for her, yet sometimes she'd tell me that she felt insecure because all of her friends were accomplishing these great things and she wasn't. She said that she was afraid she'd never have the same opportunities to explore what she wanted to become, as many people do while in college, because she was taking care of her mom 24/7. She had a bit of a complex when people would ask her what she was up to, feeling ashamed that she couldn't say she was attending some fancy school or working some great job. Over time, however, Lauren began to realize that she was doing the greatest work of any of us. She was learning to think like God thinks. That means always serving—not looking for recognition and praise, but really just letting go and serving. Lauren embodied this during the years she cared for her mother.

Dad always taught me that when you let go into service, the universe will return the favor a thousandfold. This is true in Lauren's life today. She's now living in Europe, working in the field that she's most passionate about, which is art and art production. My best friend has a sense of compassion and understanding that is far beyond her years. And just in case you were wondering, a month after Lorraine passed away, Lauren and I booked a one-way ticket to Europe and spent three months traveling around, spreading Lorraine's ashes and toasting her life and beautiful soul along the way. And given the amount of amazingly crazy and wonderful experiences Lauren and I had while we were there, we knew her mom was with us every step of the way.

Having lost both of her parents (and all of her grandparents) by the age of 22, Lauren could have given up. She might have decided that those losses would always hold her back, but that's not what she's done. She could cry every night over her past history, but she doesn't. Sure, there are times when she looks back on her life with her parents and feels sad. But she allows those wounds to be present, so they can be understood and accepted. Accepting her past has allowed her to transform her sadness into beautiful memories—memories she can recall fondly. She recently told me that she felt grateful for all that she has learned from her life so far.

My best friend has a maturity and understanding that is far beyond that of her peers. Tragedy struck her life, but she took ownership of it so that it couldn't own her. Lauren understands, as Jean-Paul Sartre put it so perfectly, that "freedom is what you do with what has been done to you." She let go of her personal history and moved forward so that she could live fully present in the now.

Giving up our personal history means making peace with the past, like Lauren has done. It means trusting that everything has happened for a reason, to teach us something important about ourselves and our lives. All of the negative experiences we've had have helped shape us into the people we are today. If we're still living in our past experiences, we aren't getting the lessons they are meant to teach us. We aren't evolving; we're staying aligned with the energy of what happened. As a result, we don't move and grow into the future. The antidote is to accept the past for what it was—and move on from it. To move away from that energy and allow ourselves to have new experiences.

As my dad taught me, the wake does not drive the boat, it is merely the trail left behind. What propels the boat forward is the energy it's putting forth right now. The same goes for our lives. Our current energy and state of being is what creates the life we are living now. Our past, just like the wake of a ship, does not drive us forward. It's merely the trail that is left behind.

Our personal history does not determine what happens in our lives now. We are the writers of our own stories, the directors of our own lives. If we're living in the past, we are just replaying the same old tapes over and over again. To be rid of past pain, and to move forward from the energy of past events, we need to choose to live in the now. Whatever our history—whatever our parents did, whatever poor choices we made, whatever mistakes or failures we've experienced—real life is happening now.

This same idea applies to forgiving ourselves for things we may have done or caused in the past. We cannot move forward and heal if we're still angry or upset or judging choices we may have made. We have to forgive ourselves in order to move forward with our lives. Focusing on things that have happened to us or decisions we regret making does not serve. Guilt, self-hatred, and shame are only destructive. As the saying goes, "Holding on to anger is like drinking poison and expecting someone else to die."

Coming Back to the Present

The opposite of people who live in the past are those who are focused on the future, and that includes me. Sometimes I have a hard time leaving my house because I want to make sure I'm entirely prepared. *What if it gets cold and I need a sweater? What if it rains? Maybe I should check the weather report and see if I should wear my boots . . .* I could go on and on in my head with thoughts like these—all of which are based in the future, and are not serving me in the moment.

I often allow my mind to obsess over things that may or may not happen at a later date. And recently one of my best friends, Ashley, called me on it. "You're always living in the future," she said, "talking about what may or may not happen. Start enjoying what you have now."

"What do you mean?" I asked, surprised (and embarrassed) that I talked about the future enough for my friends to notice it.

"You're planning our lunch when we just sat down for breakfast!" she pointed out. "Just enjoy breakfast. Lunch will happen when it happens, and it will all work out. If it doesn't, who cares?"

I am so grateful to her for naming this habit of mine. Her words have stayed with me—I really *do* plan lunch at breakfast! What's more, I get really anxious when I do. My husband has pointed out the same thing. After an argument one evening, he told me that he has a hard time doing nice things for me, because I immediately seem to ask, "What's next?" He said it doesn't appear that I appreciate his actions for very long.

Thank goodness I have people in my life who are willing to point this out—and that I'm willing to listen! For me, it can be a real struggle to live in the now. But when I'm able to do it, I notice that the tightness in my chest melts away. I find I can actually enjoy what I'm doing and feel grateful for it.

One of the practices I have started doing to stay more present is to notice my environment. I say a silent "Thank you" before I eat, and I offer a silent "God bless you" to people I pass on the street who look like they need it. This small exercise helps me be more present. And if on occasion I forget to say thank you before I eat, I don't worry about it either. That would just have me spin out into guilt—which would take me back to the past, rather than keeping me present.

I believe that what we do now is what we get later, so we create our next moments by our behavior in the present. Sometimes I get so worried about the future that I'm not even being the type of person I want to be right now. I'll catch myself snapping at someone, because in my mind I'm engaged in a big debate that hasn't even happened yet. I end up allowing the energy of that imaginary debate to manifest into my actions in the present. How crazy! When I live in the now, I find that I appreciate the beauty of what I have. When I'm present, I behave in a better way. When I do better in this moment, I receive more and better in the next. It all starts with being present.

The other day, my whole family and I were sitting around the dinner table, eating and talking and telling stories and laughing. I had been reminding myself to live in the now, so I took a moment to look around and notice each person, and I gave a silent "Thank you" for being able to sit with my family and have dinner with all of them, who I love so very much. While I was doing this I almost began to cry, but I caught myself so that I wouldn't look like a creep at the table. I was so overcome with love and gratitude for each of these people in my life, and I only realized it when I took a moment to look at each of them and be fully present in the moment.

A Better Future for Us All

I think that sometimes souls sign up to come to Earth to teach others about love or forgiveness or kindness. Even though it doesn't make sense to us at the time, it is all part of a Divine plan. We are all connected. All of us came from the same invisible force, the force that created us—and we are connected through it to each other. I call this invisible connection "consciousness."

We have our own individual consciousness, but we also have a collective consciousness made up of all the people on the planet. That means that what we do and feel affects other people. When we are filled with shame, hate, or anger, we not only create a vortex of negative energy in our own consciousness, we put it into the collective consciousness as well. We are literally increasing the negative energy around us, since negative energy generates negative energy.

On the other hand, when we love ourselves and allow ourselves to heal, we dissolve the negativity in our own consciousness and benefit the whole world in the process. When we unconditionally love ourselves, we attract others into our lives who are able to love us without conditions. If we attempt to find love outside of ourselves, without directing love toward ourselves, we will always fail. We cannot receive from others what we haven't given to ourselves.

When we give up our attachments to events from the past, we can offer love, acceptance, and forgiveness; this allows us to let go and live in the present. The result is that we not only heal ourselves, but we have a healing impact on the planet as well. Some of the people I meet at Dad's conferences tell me that they are very spiritual people, but their lives are in shambles. It seems to me that many of these individuals are very sincere, and they do what they can to offer love and acceptance toward those around them. The problem is, they aren't able to do the same for themselves. Inside they are filled with shame or guilt or fear, which translates into lives that aren't working.

If we are directing love and peace outward, but not inward toward ourselves, we are not really living spiritual lives at all. If we want to have lives filled with love, we must start with ourselves. Part of that may start with loving our past. Accepting it for everything it has been, without judging or hating any part of it. When we can do this, we can create a life in the present that is exactly what we want it to be. When we live in the present, we are able to use the greatest gift we have been given. As Einstein said, "Imagination is everything. It is the preview of life's coming attractions. Imagination is more important that knowledge."

When you imagine the events of your personal history over and over again, you continually relive them in the now. When you can live in the present and imagine how you would like to feel or what you would like your life to look like, you encounter unlimited possibilities.

WAYNE'S RESPONSE

I abhor the concept of "failure." I never, ever wanted any of my children to think of themselves as having failed at anything, and that was my motivation for making the title of this chapter one of my top ten secrets for success and inner peace. As Serena heard me say on countless occasions, "There is no failure, only feedback—everything that you do produces a result. My only concern for you is what you do with the results you produce, rather than labeling yourself as a failure and then having to live with that label."

I have noticed throughout my lifetime that so many people get stuck in the present because they are convinced that what they did or failed to do in the past is a prescription that they are consigned to follow forever. I did not want my children to place any limitations on themselves because of their own personal history. Throughout their lives I would remind them that today is not the first day of the rest of their lives, as the popular saying goes. I would tell them assertively that this is the *only* day of their lives, so they ought to take time to drink it all in and be present.

Many mornings I would enter the children's bedrooms and provide their wake-up message, singing in a booming voice, "Oh, what a beautiful morning! Gosh, what a beautiful day! I've got a beautiful feeling, everything's going my way!" Then I would tell them, "This is the only day of your life. There is no past, there is no future, there is only *now*—so go out and fully enjoy this day."

The kids would all grumble about their crazy father, but it was important to me that they know and understand the message that Emily Dickinson offered with these five well-considered words, "Forever—is composed of Nows." Such a simple yet very profound idea, and one that I wanted Serena and all of her siblings to grasp and live fully.

"You can't get out of now," I would regularly remind them. "Enjoy this day, this moment. Don't use a statement like, 'I'm not good at math,' or 'I'm clumsy,' or 'I'm not popular'—all based on something that happened in the past—as a reason for not excelling today in math, or not participating in a sporting event, or continuing to label yourself as shy or afraid. Instead, erase that personal history, and see your life today as a blank slate that you can fill in any way that you choose."

Serena mentioned the wake of the boat as a metaphor for how to give up her personal history. The wake is simply a trail that is left behind, and it is impossible for that wake to be driving the boat that that is your very life.

This message of giving up one's personal history is something that I too have had to work on throughout my lifetime. In the story that Serena told in this chapter concerning the separation that took place between her parents back in 2001, I was challenged to live in such a manner as to become fully engaged in the now. After a brief period of emotional barrenness, I pulled myself out of what I thought was the shipwreck of my life, and I let it all go. *This is now,* I would remind myself. *I can change the way I look at all of this, and what I look at will change* . . . and so it did. I saw this obstacle as a part of my own dharma, and I used my despondency to elevate my life into a new way of being.

This was truly a quantum moment in my life, which I write about in my latest book, *I Can See Clearly Now.* I was able to make the shift to new dimensions of my own spirituality by giving up my attachments to my past, reminding myself of what I was regularly reminding my children: that I had not failed, I had produced a result, and I could do whatever I chose with the results I've produced. The outcome of my giving up my personal history is that I moved into an even higher level of compassion and spiritual awakening in my writing and in my own personal life as well. I used this low point in my life to help me generate the energy to propel myself to a higher and more enlightened place.

I've often said to my children that "true nobility is not about being better than someone else, it's about being better than you used to be." This has been true for me in a very big way—indeed, I am better than I used to be, but only because I refused to any longer label myself as a failure. This involved completely and emphatically giving up my personal history and treating it as feedback, rather than as a blueprint for how the rest of my life was going to be lived.

I love this proverb, which sums up beautifully the essence of the theme of this chapter: "The best time to plant a tree is 20 years ago. The second best time is now."

CHAPTER 6

You Can't Solve a Problem with the Same Mind That Created It

*"The world as we have created it is a process of our thinking.
It cannot be changed without changing our thinking."*

— ALBERT EINSTEIN

In order to solve any problem, we must change our thinking, or think outside the box, to use a clichéd term. The problem is not really the problem, as confusing as that sounds, the problem is *the way we think about* the problem. So in order to come up with a solution, we must break through our old patterns.

My parents always encouraged me to look inside myself for answers to the toughest problems I faced. I learned that the more we stay connected to our source, to the God within, the more we tap into the power of intention and create the life we most want for ourselves. Looking outside of ourselves for answers, on the other hand, separates us from the power of intention. Our link to our source—God, the universe, or whatever you want to call it—begins to get rusty, which is a problem since it's only when we are aligned with source that we can get the things we want and need in life. As my dad always says—and I've repeated in this book—if we find ourselves living lives that we don't like, then we must change our thinking. If we change the way we think, everything in our lives can change.

Zig Ziglar liked to say that "happiness doesn't depend on who you are or what you have. It depends solely on what you think." I find that especially true for relationships. For example, my husband isn't with me when he's at work or I'm out of town, but my *thoughts* about him and our relationship are with me always. In other words, the way I experience Matt when I'm not with him is through my thoughts. So if I were always focusing on what's wrong with him or the relationship and storing those thoughts in my mind, that would be the way my relationship existed for me. But if I were to shift my thinking toward what I love about him, I would change the way my entire relationship exists in my mind— it would have gone from lousy to great just by changing my mind!

It seems we often forget that we love the person we're with *because* of who they are. Instead, we tend to think about them on the basis of who they used to be or who we think they *should* be. The result is we replace love with resentment. Suddenly, a relationship that could be real and alive becomes frustrating and uneasy. We have changed our relationship for the worse, simply because of how we're thinking about it. Yet *A Course in Miracles* says that a miracle is what happens when we change our perception. Just by changing the way we view something, we change the entire outcome of that situation.

Matt is always late. I mean always. A few years ago when we were newly dating, he was supposed to pick me up for a date. I was ready on time, and of course he was running late. Fifteen minutes late . . . half an hour late . . . *an hour and a half late*. Each minute he wasn't there, I inched closer toward a fit of rage. By the time he pulled into the driveway, I ran out there to scream at him about how rude and selfish he was. I could have been doing something with that hour and a half, too, but instead I was waiting for him. He sort of apologized and I eventually calmed down, but for the rest of the evening I couldn't let go of my bitterness.

This same situation continued to happen over and over. Anytime I was meeting Matt somewhere—that is, when we weren't getting ready together and I couldn't prod him along— I experienced anxiety beforehand, resentment and rage during the waiting period, and bitterness once he arrived. I began to think that his being late was actually ruining our relationship. Then it hit me: It takes two to tango. My reaction to his lateness wasn't helping, either.

I decided that from that point on, I wouldn't fly off the handle when he was late—it just wasn't worth how I ended up feeling inside. I knew that I couldn't change his tardiness, but I could change how I *responded* to his tardiness. That's exactly what I did.

Now whenever we're supposed to meet somewhere, I text him to see if he's running late. If he is, I don't leave to meet him until he lets me know that he's in the car and on his way. If we have something really important to go to, I tell him it starts an hour earlier than it does! The best part is, since he appreciates that I've been patient with him, he tries harder to be on time. And for the most part, he is! Whereas before he'd take his time if he was running late—he knew I was going to freak out, so why rush?—now he wants to be as close to on time as possible.

Clearly, I wasn't going to be able to solve the problem of my re-activity with the same mind that was being so reactive, so I learned to be more flexible. It all goes back to changing how we think. (I know—I sound like a broken record at this point!) If we don't like where we are in our lives, we must change how we think. That's the only way to get to where we'd rather be.

Revising Our Self-Talk and Memes

When we change the way we look at problems, the problems themselves transform. Generally they become more manageable, and we become more peaceful. So if you suffered from an addiction, for example, you would need to change the way you viewed that addiction. If you saw it as something that had a hold over you—something you couldn't get away from—what you'd get is more addiction.

Similarly, if you were unhappy with being overweight, you'd have to change how you think—imagining what you would like to look like at your preferred weight and setting that intention. That, by itself, would change the way you thought about food. You'd start to view your weight as something *that can change*—rather than as a characteristic you inherited from you mom or dad that cannot shift.

We must begin to believe that we are capable of change at any moment of the day. We have to view ourselves—even if it's just in our imagination—as changeable. As the brilliant metaphysics teacher and New Age author Neville Goddard wrote, "We must move mentally from thinking of the end to thinking from the end. This, reason could never do. By its nature it is restricted to the evidence of the senses; but imagination, having no such limitations, can."

If you're an addict or overweight, you need to imagine your new life in detail. What would it look and feel like? Once you can hold that vision in your mind, you may realize that in order to become free, you'll need to let go of certain friends or change your environment. In a way, changing your mind is very similar to letting go of your personal history.

If you believe you're overweight because of a problem that exists in your life—such as, *My whole family is overweight, and therefore so am I*—you must change how you think about that problem. Start by contemplating the idea that you're worth it. Then make the commitment to consume smaller portions, and to take a few more steps today than you did yesterday. Eventually, it comes down to loving yourself enough to let go of habits you don't feel good about, and to take a close look at the messages you're constantly sending to yourself.

This reminds me of when Lauren and I were on Maui with my dad one summer. We were talking about how we wanted to get into really good shape before starting our junior year of high school. Lauren said something about how going on a diet was really hard, and I said I didn't like to work out. Before we had even started our workout and diet plans, we were already talking ourselves out of it—going over and over how hard it was going to be.

Dad came over and asked us what we were doing. We told him we were coming up with our summer fitness plans, but it wasn't going so well. We talked about how hard dieting and exercise were, and that neither one of us wanted to spend our summer doing anything difficult.

My dad just looked at us as if we were aliens from another planet—a familiar look, which usually signaled that we were about to be given some big lesson. He said that we were just repeating "memes," and that none of what we were saying was true unless we decided it was. A meme, he explained, is an idea that is passed on from person to person, even generation to generation. He said that a meme is really like a mind virus; it infiltrates, takes over, and spreads. Neither Lauren nor I had deep personal experience with exercise and fitness, after all. We were just repeating ideas and beliefs—memes—that we'd heard from other people.

The word *meme* was created by the biologist Richard Dawkins to describe "a unit of cultural transmission, or a unit of imitation" and meant to evoke the idea of a gene. Basically, a meme is a concept that gets lodged in our memory, determining habitual ways of behaving. In most cultures, eating breakfast is a meme, for example. All social customs are actually memes—they're things we find ourselves doing because we have been culturally conditioned to do them. Memes are not necessarily bad—unless they perpetuate thoughts that lead to behaviors we don't want.

Once I discovered the meaning of a meme, I realized how often people use them. Think about how often we hear "Life is hard," "Healthy eating is difficult," or "Losing weight is always a struggle." These things *can* be difficult—but they can also be easy. If you make up your mind that losing weight is really important to you, then finding the time to work out and eat well will be a breeze. You'll surround yourself with supportive people and motivational messages. And since you've aligned yourself with positive energy, that's what you'll find in your life.

I notice that people often reply, "Not bad," when asked how they're doing. Rather than associate my state with feeling bad,

I choose to align with feeling good. So I say, "I feel fabulous," or "I feel wonderful," or "I'm doing great." I'm choosing a meme that gets me closer to the feeling state I desire.

You've probably heard someone say, "Wow, that house is really nice, but I could never afford something like that." Not a meme I choose to invite into my world! Instead, I say, "I can definitely picture myself living there with my wonderful husband and kids." This isn't about just saying optimistic things; it's about changing the way we look at life. We're learning to do as Neville said and operate from a space that is supportive of our dreams and desires.

When we believe in something enough, we make it true for ourselves. We create it in our lives, whether or not it's something we want. Nowhere is this more prevalent (and detrimental) than in man-woman relating. It's a going theme among the women I know that "men are jerks" and "it's hard to find a good one." I have never believed this, and I have never repeated these memes. I choose to think that you attract the type of person that you yourself are. I believe that I am great, so I assume the men I meet are going to be great, too. To my women friends, I say that if you regularly attract mean guys, look at the type of person you are. You have to *be* the kind of person you want to meet. (That's a meme too—a good one!)

In order to revise our negative messages and memes, we must "unlearn what we have already learned," as Yoda said. If we want to keep from handing negative memes down to future generations, we must take care with what we say to our children. Our kids will end up believing the memes we feed them, and the result is entire generations with limited beliefs about life. They'll have expectations before they're old enough to come to conclusions on their own.

Changing our use of memes is part of changing the way we think. Notice which memes you use in your everyday life and language, and start replacing the negative memes with positive ones. That way, you can use memes to *solve* the issues in your life, rather than re-creating beliefs and situations you no longer want.

Be Still and Tune in to Your Soul

Thinking differently starts with the experience of momentary stillness. This stillness whispers to me. It says, "You are a beautiful person. Keep it up." It says, "You are deeply and profoundly loved—pass it on." It reminds me, "You are infinite perfection. Let others know that they are, too. Everything you want and need is already on its way. Tell everyone you meet." I don't experience this stillness when I doubt myself, feel ashamed of myself, or go against what I know my highest self wants. In fact, when I choose such self-sabotaging thoughts, the stillness I have seems to go away.

I have asked this stillness in the past, "Why, when I am in a dark place and struggling, do you leave me?" The answer is always the same: "You asked me to leave." This I know is true. As Deepak Chopra says, "To make the right choices in life, you have to get in touch with your soul. To do this, you need to experience solitude, which most people are afraid of, because in the silence you hear the truth and know the solutions."

We always have the choice between loving ourselves and feeling ashamed. When we choose to do things that cause us shame, or choose to feel ashamed because others tell us to, the Divine presence in each of us takes a backseat. It sends the wrong message to the universe. If I choose to get really drunk and embarrass myself, for instance, then I'm asking the universe to give me more experiences of shame and embarrassment.

When I feel insecure or ashamed or jealous, I don't know how to offer others acceptance and love. It isn't that I don't want to, but when bitterness takes over it's really hard, almost impossible, to find the love inside to offer to others. It's as if it isn't even there for me to give away. When I feel happy, on the other hand, the universe provides me with love and acceptance for those around me. I find I want everyone to know that they are loved and accepted as they are.

Eventually, it comes down to loving ourselves enough to get rid of whatever we don't feel good about in life. Remembering that I am worthy of change and deserve something better helps propel me forward whenever I'm struggling to let go of something that isn't good for me, be it a relationship or some aspect of my behavior. When I begin to contemplate myself as worthy of something more, I find the desire to change so strong that nothing can stop me.

I used to be really jealous when someone would tell me they were living in New York City and working at their dream job. I wanted to be doing something similar, but I had no idea what my dream job even *was*. Then one day it clicked for me. I was thinking about my career from a space of envy and frustration, so I wasn't viewing others' success from a space of love and joy. When I shifted my mind-set, things started to shift for me as well. I was able to let go of my envy when I realized that the people I envied had taken a leap of faith to move to NYC in the first place. They had taken on the risk of failure. When I realized that it was my own fear of failure that held me back, I no longer felt envious of my friends for going after their dreams—I felt like I wanted to join them! I wanted to be as brave as they had been.

I began to daydream all day long about the success *I* wanted—the life I wanted to be living. Before I went to bed, I would imagine how it would feel if everything worked out just as I dreamed it would, and I'd drift off to sleep with that feeling in my body. As a result, I truly felt excited for other people when they told me they were working toward their dreams or following their passion. I was excited for them because I truly believed it was going to happen for me soon, too—and then it did! Similarly, I had been afraid of writing and sharing my innermost self with people. But then one day, I just started to write, and I wasn't afraid anymore.

There is something Sara Blakely, the founder of Spanx, said that I absolutely love and agree with: "I think very early on in life we all learn what we're good at and what we're not good at, and we stay where it's safe." We stay doing what we know we're good at because the risk of failing is scary. Once I was able to get past the fear of not measuring up, or the fear of failing, I was able to contemplate having things show up in my life that before seemed impossible.

Pushing myself to try things that were scary has made me a more compassionate and understanding person. Now if I meet someone who exhibits qualities I admire, I'm not envious; instead, I want to learn from them. I've come back to a place of love, by quieting my ego and listening to my soul.

When we love ourselves, love is what we have to give away. When we are insecure or frustrated with ourselves, insecurity and frustration are what we have to give. We cannot give away what we don't have, after all. I meet people all the time who are so insecure or upset or frustrated with themselves and their lives that they cannot be happy for anyone else. Or they *pretend* to be happy for others, but inside are condemning, jealous, or bitter. Secretly they may be judging that the person doesn't deserve their good fortune, or hoping it won't last forever. People who are living from this place are not bad or evil; they're simply lacking love for themselves. They do not know how to create the lives they want for themselves, and all they have to offer are the feelings of lack they're experiencing inside.

Many people have said to me, "Of course it's easy for you to follow your passion—you have wealthy parents who would never let you end up on the street." Their thinking often goes like this: *I have bills to pay and mouths to feed. I can't just quit my job to pursue my dreams.* When I hear this, I always think, *No one is telling you to quit your job! There are many ways to start following your dreams, even while paying the bills.* After all, my dad wrote his first book, *Your Erroneous Zones,* while he was still a professor. He wrote it while on *vacation!* He was following his passion and focusing on what he ultimately wanted to do, which was to write. When you have a passion, the drive comes naturally, and you align with the abundant nature of the universe.

Aligning with the Energy of God

Several years ago I created a vision board. A vision board is a visual representation of the life you desire—a poster or bulletin board you cover with words and images that describe the way you want to feel, the people you want around you, and the specific circumstances you most want for your life. I placed my board where I could see it regularly, reminding myself daily about what I wanted to attract.

I included images of the kind of person I wanted to be as well as material things I wanted. I was blown away by the response I got from some people when they saw that I had included material items—I got a lot of judgment about that. But my take is that wanting material things does not cancel out one's spiritual pursuits. I refuse to apologize for wanting abundance in my life. Material things and spirituality are not mutually exclusive things!

Back to the vision board. I knew I wouldn't get the experiences I was asking for simply because I wanted them. I had to *become* them—to align myself with their energy. If I wanted God to give me abundance and love and kindness and generosity, I needed to offer those things to people I met. I needed to align myself with the energy of God, which is always serving, always giving, and always loving.

When I made this my priority, I began to shift the way I behaved. I changed the way I viewed people and the world. I also shifted the way I thought—which was the hardest change of all. Being a young woman in my 20s, I had a bad habit of talking about famous people, and not always in the nicest of ways. I knew gossiping didn't make me feel good; I would often say a little prayer in my head for the person we were talking about. But once I created my vision board, I took my dislike for gossip from an internal to an external experience. I simply stopped participating.

I remember a friend talking about how much she hated a particular celebrity. When she asked me what I thought, I did not engage. I said I didn't know them, so I couldn't really say. This didn't mean I didn't have a preference for or against this person's purported behavior—giving up gossip doesn't mean you give up your opinions. It just means you stop spreading more negativity by talking about them.

The world is as it should be. The economy is the way it is, and people behave the way they behave. When we get angry about things that are beyond our control, we contribute to the pollution of anger. Those who are already behaving in ways that are removed from God do not need to be judged or condemned for their behavior. No amount of anger or disgust is going to motivate someone to change. People change through love.

I came to realize that if I allowed myself to be upset or offended by society or the behavior of others—or if I judged them for judging me—I was only doubling the amount of judgment in my space. Instead, I chose to stay connected to my source. As a result, I began to radiate a higher energy. This can happen for you, too. Once you align with God, people will experience your love and light wherever you go. Problems will simply not be able to flourish in your presence.

If we spend the majority of our energy dissecting other people's lives or criticizing other people for the way they are, we are actually taking away from our own ability to attract what we want into our lives. Not only is our energy focused on others' lives and behaviors, but we're applying all of our energy to thoughts of criticism and condemnation. That will only bring more of those energies into our own lives.

The Courage to Follow Your Dreams

My brother Sands is passionate about surfing. He loves the ocean more than anything—in fact, he was named for it! He just graduated from college and isn't sure what he wants to do with his life, but he knows he wants it to involve the ocean.

The last time I was on Maui, I overheard Dad telling my brother that whatever he decides to do for work, he should make sure he is passionate about it. Dad said, "If you want to surf for the rest of your life, figure out a way to make surfing work for you so that you can do what you are passionate about and get paid for it."

I was so happy when I heard him say that, and so grateful to have the father I have. I can only imagine how many times young people have told their parents that they want to surf or paint or dance for a living, and their parents have replied, "There's no money in that—give it up and get a real job." I was really proud that my dad told my brother not to give up on his passion, but to follow that passion to success.

Recently, Sands has also become slightly fanatical about playing golf. Mom constantly tells him that he should hire an instructor and eventually go pro, since he's so good at it. Our mother doesn't pay attention to the fact that Sands just started playing, and most people who turn professional have been practicing their entire lives. She believes in him so much that she doesn't see any limitations to his potential success. It is so beautiful to watch how much our parents love and believe in all of us!

Everyone has dreams and passions, of course. The people I meet who seem the most happy and content in their lives tend to be the ones who are doing what they love. It isn't about success for these people, although success is great, too. It's more about getting to live the life they desire.

Like my brother, when deciding what passion to make your life's goal, you may want to consider whether it is natural for you— whether you have the inherent skill set for it. I use this phrase because a lot of people have dreams that aren't natural to them. For example, I am not a great dancer. (Okay, I'm probably more in the "terrible" category.) My friends and siblings will happily point that out whenever I hit the dance floor I look a *little* better than Elaine from *Seinfeld,* but not much.

Since I know I'm not a great dancer, I'm kind of obsessed with people who are. I have a secret dream of being an amazing dancer; being on a stage and having incredible rhythm and moves. But am I going to pursue this dream? Probably not. Not because I can't learn, but because it just isn't natural to me. Getting up on a stage and speaking in front of thousands of people, on the other hand? For me, that's a breeze.

Luckily, I love public speaking—it's a dream worth pursuing. If I tried to pursue dance and based my sense of self-worth on how I did in that area, I would end up feeling pretty bad. Instead of focusing on what I *can't* do, I focus on what I can—what makes me feel good about myself—and I go after that. As Albert Einstein said, "Everybody is a genius. But if you judge a fish by its ability to climb a tree, it will live its whole life believing that it is stupid."

If you have a dream of being a famous singer but are terrified of being in front of an audience, perhaps singing isn't the right thing for you. This doesn't mean you can't be in the music industry, however. Maybe you're meant to be an incredible songwriter or pianist or producer. Of course if you have a phenomenal voice but also have stage fright, that doesn't mean your dream is doomed. You can still be a successful singer—you simply have to apply yourself to facing the fear and overcoming it. You have to figure out what you're willing to overcome to make your passion natural for you, and then you have to go for it.

If you allow anything to stop you from pursuing your passion, you're stopping your soul from expanding. I have found that when I'm serving others—and even encouraging others to follow their dreams—God gives me back more of whatever it is I want. When I'm critical of others' dreams, and insulting, condescending, or judgmental of them, I feel myself drift away from my source—and away from my own dreams as well.

When you encounter a friend, family member, or acquaintance who puts you down, insults your ideas, or makes fun of you, remind yourself that it's *your* dream, not theirs. I try to say a little prayer for people like that and let them go. If I can't avoid them or get away from them, I don't share my dreams with them. In fact, I often tell friends and acquaintances to use caution when talking about their dreams with others. I say this because so many of us live from a place of fear that dreamers may get negative reactions from the well-meaning people in their lives. It's all too easy to let fearful loved ones talk you out of what you need to do to make your dream come true.

Spanx is now a billion-dollar industry that Sara Blakely founded on her own. (I love the fact that she listened to my dad's tapes as a teenager and credits the lessons he taught to some of her success.) She has said of her original idea, "I made a conscious decision not to tell anyone in my life. Now I tell people—don't tell anyone your idea until you have invested enough of yourself in it that you are not going to turn back. When a person has an idea at that conception moment it is the most vulnerable—one negative comment could knock you off course."

If Sara would have shared her idea for Spanx with her friends or family, and they told her all the reasons why it wouldn't work, she may never have even started. Her billion-dollar company is now employing hundreds of people and funding schools in Africa. It is so successful that it allowed her to join the Giving Pledge, in which she promised to give at least half of her wealth during her lifetime to philanthropy and charitable organizations around the world.

As I've mentioned, my biggest fear in life is not living my dream. Back when I was in law school, I was standing on the edge of living someone else's dream. As hard as it was, I knew that if I chose to keep going like this, I wouldn't be able to face myself in the mirror. I am so grateful to myself that I decided to be loyal to my own intuition. I am in awe of how the universe conspires to help me achieve success—success I never could have expected.

Today I realize more than ever that living my own destiny is a choice. I can also choose to allow my life to pass me by, or to blame others for holding me back. But I truly understand that my past does not define me. The decisions I have made up until this point do not determine the decisions I make going forward. If I start to feel stuck, I know I need to come up with a different way of thinking.

If you find yourself wanting to follow your dreams but are afraid, assume the feeling you would experience if they came true. This isn't about thinking about what you want; it is about *feeling* it in your body. Act as if what you want is already on its way, and trust that it is. Then let go and watch what happens. That's what I do—and it has worked for me so far!

WAYNE'S RESPONSE

The essential message of this chapter is something I spent a great deal of time attempting to get across to all of my children, and that is: Always remain flexible. Be willing to change and eliminate any and all attachments to one particular way of thinking and being. I love this observation written by one of the most influential mentors in my own life, the transcendent Ralph Waldo Emerson: "I wish to say what I think and feel today, with the proviso that tomorrow perhaps I shall contradict it all." Emerson is encouraging us to keep an open mind, and be willing to change even long-held and cherished ideas.

When one of my sons or daughters would talk to me about a specific problem they were facing with their health or even their relationships, I would ask them to examine what kind of a mind-set they were employing that created the difficulty. "If you are believing that your particular point of view is unassailable, and it was that very same point of view that contributed to the problem you're facing, then you must let go of your attachment to your point of view."

So many times the problems that my children were experiencing were the result of needing to be right, and consequently making the other person wrong. In the case of Serena's husband always being late, I would say to her, "You're saying to me that you have a right to be miserable because of his inconsiderate tardiness. Why not try this approach: When you have a choice to be right or to be kind, try picking kind and see if that might make a difference, not only in his always being unpunctual, but in your own feelings as well." At first Serena held on to her position of being right, but as she began to shift her thinking and then her behavior, the problem was solved. She became more peaceful, and that is all any of us really, truly want—simply to have inner peace and contentment. It is always a choice.

I would regularly remind the children that their concept of themselves is nothing more than all of the things that they believe to be true. And if what they believe to be true is helping them create situations in which they are unhappy or even unhealthy, they are then challenged to change what they have unwaveringly held on to as an absolute truth. This is very difficult for most people to do, and this is why so many stay stuck, because they would rather be right than happy. They would rather defend their right to be miserable rather than admit that their intransigence is what is causing them to be upset or even immobilized.

One of the wisest books ever written was dictated over 2,500 years ago by the spiritual master Lao-tzu: the Tao Te Ching. I spent an entire year of my life reading and putting into practice the wisdom of these 81 verses, and wrote a book about my year as a practicing Taoist titled *Change Your Thoughts, Change Your Life*. The 76nd verse of the Tao begins with these words, which are so applicable to the message of this chapter of Serena's writing:

> *A man is born gentle and weak;*
> *at his death he is hard and stiff.*
> *All things, including the grass and trees,*
> *are soft and pliable in life;*
> *dry and brittle in death.*
>
> *Stiffness is thus a companion of death;*
> *flexibility a companion of life.*

"By remaining inflexible and rigid, a little portion of you dies," I always told my children. It is so much more joyful to be a companion of life by remaining pliable and soft.

CHAPTER 7

There Are No Justified Resentments

"If you judge people, you have no time to love them."
— Anonymous

Growing up, there was a five letter word beginning with a "b" that we were not allowed to say or use. No, I'm not talking about *bitch;* the real bad word in our household was *blame.* Dad has a zero-tolerance policy for resentment. He simply would not allow any of us to place blame on anyone or anything other than ourselves.

"You are the product of all the choices you have made," he would say.

"But you don't understand!" I'd complain. "My math teacher really hates me, and I know it. She makes me mad every day."

"She can't make you mad," he'd reply. "You *allow* yourself to be mad by the way you process what she says to you. No one can make you feel inferior or unloved, or hurt your feelings, without your permission and consent. You are the one who sets the boundaries. You can free yourself. Start today."

Even though I felt exasperated by his crazy logic, Dad never wavered. In order to be completely free, he'd tell me, we have to take responsibility for everything that is going on in our life—even the things we don't like. This doesn't mean we're at "fault" for what we don't like; it just means that if we want to be free from it, we must take responsibility for it. Once we do this, we can change—rather than expecting someone or something else to change for us.

My dad tells this great story from back when he was a practicing psychologist. He had a patient who would come in every week and spend the entire hour bashing her mother, blaming her for everything that had gone wrong in her life. Around their fourth session, Dad said to the woman, "So basically what you're saying is that all of the decisions you've made in your life—the decisions that have gotten you to where you are now, which is a place you don't like—are your mother's fault."

The woman nodded yes, agreeing that her mother was to blame for all the problems that currently existed in her life. Dad replied, "If your mother is the real source of all of your problems, as you're saying, then bring her in. I'll treat your mother, and you will get better."

I love this story because it shows how easy it is to place blame on someone else, when what we really need to do is take responsibility ourselves. I often hear others say things like, "I won't change for anyone" or "This is the way I am, take it or leave it." I try to steer clear of anyone who would say anything like that. I prefer to spend my time with people who want to evolve, grow, and expand their consciousness—people who are taking responsibility for who they are and their impact on the world. Just like my dad taught me to do.

What's in a Label?

When I was a kid, Dad loved to make a big, dramatic scene when I wanted to be right—which was all the time. One of my very favorite memories happened when I was in first grade. I came home from school really upset because a boy in my class had called me stupid in front of everybody.

Now, I imagine most fathers would have consoled their six-year-old daughters, assuring them that they weren't stupid and the boy was wrong and mean. Not mine.

"You must have believed this boy if you made his opinion of you more important than your own opinion of yourself," Dad said. "Do *you* think you're stupid?"

"No," I replied. "I'm super smart!"

"Well, what if tomorrow this boy comes into class and says, 'Yesterday, Serena, you were stupid, and today you are a car'? Would that make you a car?"

Of course I started cracking up at the thought being a car—how ridiculous! Dad got Sands and Saje involved, even though they were only four and two years old at the time. He got them down on all fours playing "car," saying, "Serena, you're a car! This little boy said so!" I thought the whole thing was so funny. All of us were laughing, and even though I was pretty young, what he was implying made perfect sense.

That day, my dad taught me an important lesson. Just because someone puts a label on me, that doesn't mean it's true. It says nothing about who I am; if anything, it says something about *them*. It's my belief that if parents would teach this to children at a young age, bullying would become much less prevalent because name-calling would no longer have such an effect. I was the scrawniest little kid in class, but I had the most confidence of anyone. I knew that what other people thought or said about me was none of my business.

Interestingly, letting go of others' opinions was easier for me when I was younger than it is now. I'm still confident about who I am, but not all my plans have entirely panned out. Back when I was in school, if someone asked me what I did for a living, I simply told them I was getting my master's. It seemed to earn me some respect. But after I got my degree, I didn't start a career right away. When people would ask me what I was doing, I felt embarrassed to admit I wasn't sure yet. I had become so used to seeing my value as a person tied to what I was "doing." When I was doing nothing, I felt that I *was* nothing. All of the great parenting and confidence building I received as a young person did not prevent me from feeling this way.

Thankfully, in writing this book I have reconnected with myself. I have begun to see how pointless all of my negative thoughts really were. No one else was putting this pressure on me or making me feel this way; I was *choosing* to feel insecure. I can't really explain why I would choose to feel bad, but I noticed myself shy away from things that I knew would make me feel better. I was down, and looking for more reasons to stay down.

One day it clicked that I could go back to being the confident, happy, carefree girl that I so fondly remembered being. From that day forward, whenever I was faced with a decision between something that would make me feel good about myself and something that would make me feel bad, I chose to feel good. This could have been deciding not to have a second glass of wine at dinner, or not picking a stupid fight with my husband. Other times it was choosing to stay in at night because I needed to get some writing done—when I write, I feel fulfilled in a way that partying can't touch.

I realized that if I wanted to feel good and light and peaceful, I needed to make choices that would help me align with feeling those things. How we feel about ourselves is a choice. This was what Dad was teaching us with his zero-tolerance policy on blame. Blaming others—or ourselves—makes us feel worse, not better. Instead, we must choose what feels good. For me, this means looking for opportunities to love and understand and forgive, to align with the type of situations I really want in life. I decided to stop blaming myself for not being further along in my career than I was. Instead, I started to focus on loving myself and accepting my life exactly as it was. At that point, my life started to change for the better.

Dana's Story

I believe that we don't forgive for anyone else's sake but our own. Choosing to forgive those who have wronged us is something we do for ourselves, once we've decided that we're ready to heal. It helps us regain the power that someone else has over our emotional well-being, and is in fact the most generous thing we can do for ourselves. I love this Mark Twain quote that my dad often repeats: "Forgiveness is the fragrance that the violet sheds on the heel that has crushed it."

When I think about forgiveness, one woman immediately comes to mind. Dana Liesegang and I met on a cruise I went on with Dad in January 2012, and she immediately stood out for two reasons. First, I met her on the dance floor. She seemed around my age and was dancing like crazy, having the best time. Second, she was in a wheelchair.

I wanted to know more about her, so I asked if she wanted to come to dinner the next night with me. She agreed. As we ate, Dana told me how she came to be in the wheelchair. When she was 18 years old, she joined the Navy so she could see the world and get out of her small hometown. Shortly after joining, however, her life felt off track. She was partying hard and drinking a lot, going in a negative direction fast.

One night, Dana walked off base to mail a postcard to her boyfriend. As she was walking back, a guy who was also in the Navy offered to give her a ride. Dana got in the car and noticed an empty Jack Daniel's bottle, but since the guy was driving fine, she ignored it. But it wasn't long before Dana heard a voice—God, her own intuition, whatever you want to call it—tell her loud and clear that she needed to get out of that car. She was too scared to follow the voice, and her fear ultimately changed the course of her entire life.

The man drove to the top of a cliff and stopped the car. Dana got out and said she had to pee, and as she walked away from the car, the guy followed her and asked if she'd ever had someone watch her pee before. She tried to get away from him, but unfortunately she couldn't. The guy choked her, raped her, threw her 70 feet over the edge of the cliff, and left her to die.

Dana woke up a few weeks later in the hospital, on a respirator, paralyzed from the neck down. She spent months there, devastated and scared, still in shock over what had happened to her.

A short while before, she'd been a free-spirited party girl; now she was confined to a hospital bed.

The rapist was ultimately kicked out of the Navy but otherwise went unpunished (until years later when he was arrested and put in jail for kidnapping a woman). The Navy promised to take care of Dana for the rest of her life as long as she kept quiet—but after 18 years of silence, she decided that she was no longer going to live in fear and was starting to share her story.

Unbelievably, Dana told me that getting raped and thrown off of a cliff was the best thing that ever happened to her. She was no longer upset or angry about what happened; she actually considered it a *gift*. Her life before the Navy had been very difficult: She lived with six different parents by the time she was 10 and was molested at age 14, and she was set to continue the cycle she had known, of alcohol and violence. The attack she suffered forced her to wake up and start living her life from a more spiritual place.

Being with Dana that night impacted me deeply. Not just because of the tragedy of her story and the horrors she had endured, but because of the unbelievable light and beauty that radiated off of her in spite of it all. I began a friendship with her right then and there, keeping in close contact after the cruise.

Through a series of stem-cell transplants and her own sheer will, Dana ended up regaining the function of her neck, arms, and most of her fingers. And after our meeting, she decided to go see John of God—a healer who performs spiritual "surgeries" for a wide variety of physical and nonphysical issues. Dana received two surgeries, and shortly after that, she got some control of her colon back. This might not sound like much, but according to Dana, it was huge. She said you can't imagine what it's like not to have control over your colon until you lose it. This change was incredible for her, because it's often said that colon function is the last thing to come back after a spinal-cord injury. Although she was still in a wheelchair, she felt incredibly grateful.

A few months later, Dana came on another cruise where Dad was speaking. He told her story to the audience, and then he called her up onstage—and to everyone's shock and amazement,

Dana *walked* up to meet him! I couldn't believe that this amazing woman, who had been told she would never again move from the neck down, was actually doing this. I had tears in my eyes and chills in my whole body as I watched her deliberately move one foot at a time, holding on to the handrail, while every single person in that crowd stood and applauded for her.

Dana later told me that she had only seen herself moving forward since the night of her rape, and she knew she wouldn't stop until she was walking again. Amazingly, she also said that she forgave the man who had done this to her years ago. She said it was easy for her to forgive him, because she realized that she had no idea what *his* life had been like—what he had endured that would allow him do the things he had done. With tears streaming down her face, she told me that it was harder for her to forgive herself for not getting out of that car than it was to forgive her rapist. She went on to say that if she hadn't been able to forgive him—and herself—she didn't think she could be making such remarkable progress.

Of all the people I know, Dana would be the most justified in having resentments, but she doesn't. She chose to see her attack not as a tragedy, but as an opportunity. My friendship with Dana is a true blessing in my life, and I have learned so much from her. She is now focused on teaching others about the power of forgiveness and is writing her own book for Hay House. She told me that she's most excited about this because she knows how many people it will help. Dana's goal these days is to see just how many men and women she can serve by sharing her story with them.

The secret that "there are no justified resentments" does not mean we don't have the right to be angry. In fact, anger is a natural response to our boundaries being crossed. What Dana taught me is that anger does not serve us; instead, it keeps us in the same place we want to get away from. Like attracts like, so negative energy attracts more of the same. When you stay angry or upset or pissed off, you continue to attract more of that kind of experience into your life. Rather than moving forward, as Dana has always done, you continue to stay in the same place. On the other hand, when you're able to move away from the anger and frustration, you allow yourself to move away from the negative situation or person or events altogether. This is true freedom.

A Lesson Closer to Home

Meeting Dana had a profound effect on the way I view things that have happened in my own life. When she and I first met and she told me about the man who so viscously attacked her, I expected her to say that she hated him and wanted him to suffer. You can imagine how surprised I was when she said that she only sent him love. Hearing her say that made me realize that I was capable of doing the same toward those who I felt had wronged me. Dad had told me this throughout my life, and I knew how he had forgiven his father for abandoning him, but Dad was always different. Hearing it from someone else—especially someone so close to my own age—was even more impactful for me.

I take such inspiration from amazing survivors like Dana, and I endeavor to live my life in the same way they live theirs. The fact that they're survivors isn't even what moves me so deeply—it's what they *chose* to do with what's been done to them. It is their connection to the knowing that life is in Divine order and there is a plan for all of us that inspires me so much.

The tools I have learned from Mom and Dad have helped me extend forgiveness to strangers I meet or acquaintances I have, but hearing Dana's story of forgiveness helped me realize that I had been holding out on one particular person in my life who has hurt me. Some of her decisions have been painful to see, and it's also been difficult to watch how much she's hurt herself. And how much her she's hurt my whole family, especially my mom.

That person is my sister. She has battled addiction for the last 14 years, and I have watched her come close to dying several times because she just couldn't get herself to stop taking prescription drugs. Prescription-drug addiction has become an epidemic in our culture. I know this firsthand, because it's been in my own home. And while I don't think the blame lies exclusively with the medical community, I do think that they are very deeply involved in the crisis.

As a society we have to change our attitude toward pharmaceuticals. If we don't, we will have entire generations of children that are hooked on pills. Sometimes it seems to me that *Brave New World* is becoming a reality. More and more people are choosing not to feel, but instead to numb themselves. I respect pharmaceutical drugs and I know they save lives. But when they are abused, as they so often are, they can literally take someone's life. I believe these drugs, and my sister's addiction to them, have taken much of her life from her.

My sister and I are very close in age, and we grew up in the same household with the same parents. Yet for some reason, we are very different. She has struggled with addiction issues for years, and I have been struggling with not judging her for it for just as long. My sister's addiction has landed her in jail several times, not to mention in the hospital. What's so heartbreaking for me is that her only crime is harming herself.

Even though I have the understanding that we are all on our own paths, and even though I have the knowing that all I can really do is love her, it doesn't mean that doing so is always easy. I've often found myself wanting to shake her so that she'll wake up and quit the drugs. I've wanted to scream that she's wasting her life on pills and life is better when you feel things, even when what you feel is bad. I've wanted to tell her how much she's hurting me, our parents, and our entire family, but she already knows that. I know she's taken drugs because she can't handle the pain she's already caused; my yelling these things at her would not make her feel how much I love her. A drug addict's biggest crime is against themselves, after all. More than anything, I wish I could get my sister to see how perfect she is.

I believe drug addicts have a form of self-loathing that only they can understand. When I look past my sister's addiction, I see the person who is hysterically funny, incredibly intelligent, kind, and empathic. I see the early memories of my big sister who protected me and stuck up for me. I try to understand that, just as I have a path that I am on, she has one, too. I have to force myself to remember that everything is in perfect order, even though it can be extremely difficult. Honestly, there are times when it can be just too damn hard to see someone you love slowly killing themselves.

I know this issue affects so many families in this country, and it just breaks my heart. Some people decide to stop taking drugs and are able to make that decision in an instant and never look back. I believe this is an option for everyone, as long as we choose to see it that way. This may be easy for me to say because although I have definitely done my fair share of drugs, I've never been addicted to them.

One day a few years back, Mom called me and broke down. She apologized for not having been a better mother—for not having protected my sister and guided her to a different path. Mom was apologizing because the rest of us had to deal with the gut-wrenching pain of watching someone we loved hurt herself. I reassured her, saying that there was no better mother in the world (which is true), and that my sister has always been my greatest teacher. That without her in my life, I would not have learned forgiveness, understanding, and compassion at an early age. I told Mom that while I got angry and scared when my sister was in the hospital or in jail, I also understood that the only thing I could do was to love her no matter what—to make her feel that she had my unconditional love and acceptance.

I knew my parents had saved my young life once in the same way. All I could do was make my sister understand that I loved her and wanted her to be happy and safe. That by itself would mean I had fulfilled my highest calling as a God-realized human being—which is to love everyone without condition and without judgment.

There is a wise part of me that understands that judging my sister and staying resentful toward her for some of the things she's done will not serve either of us. I know that my highest self and her highest self want peace, and that by being angry at her I am depriving both of us of just that. I know that no matter what happens with her, I am a better person for knowing her, for loving her, and for being her sister—with or without the drugs. I know all of this, but it is still hard.

I have gotten to a point in my life where I acknowledge and honor when I am feeling sad, angry, depressed, or hurt. Having these feelings is okay, and I don't try to ignore them or brush them under the rug. I do not tell myself to just be positive, or to expect all of the negative feelings to go away. I honor my feelings and I bring them to light. I talk about them and give voice to them, and sometimes I write about them. I know that I am giving myself the most spiritual gift I can give when I do this.

For me, spirituality isn't about being positive and memorizing great quotes. Spirituality is honoring the truth that is within me so that I can grow and expand and improve. Feeling upset about my sister's life isn't wrong, so when I do, I don't feel ashamed for it. I try to acknowledge and even embrace it so that I don't stay stuck and dwell in it. I am also at a place where I can send her love despite it all, and I am damn proud of that, because there was a time in my life when this would have seemed impossible.

I have been able to change the way I view my sister's addiction because I have gotten to a place where I realize that I can't force her to live the way I want her to live. All I can do is love her while she goes through this journey. In doing so, I have been able to come to an understanding that she has an illness called addiction. I wouldn't hate or be angry with someone in my family who was sick with a different illness, so why do I get so angry with her? I have begun to view her life in a different way, and even though this doesn't change what she is experiencing, it certainly changes what I experience inside.

These days, my sister does appear to be doing better—she seems reconnected to her highest self and is on a path that is healthy and full of love and support.

Release and Be Free

The secret "there are no justified resentments" is about taking back control of our lives. Even if we had the worst childhood, marriage, or accident imaginable—even if we have every right to be upset—we must ask whether our resentment is working on our behalf. Just like Dana, we must ask ourselves how these feelings of hate, anger, sadness, neglect, and resentment are serving us today. Yes, we have all been wronged. Many of you reading this book have been abused, hurt, abandoned, cheated on, or treated unfairly. Moreover, there is probably a person or even a group of people you can point to who seem to have caused your distress. But unfortunately, that's not the point. Regardless of how "right" you are, your resentment is only hurting yourself.

Letting go of resentments is part of how we change the way we think—bringing the focus of our emotional state under our own control. I know how hard this can be, but it's worth it to start seeing yourself as free of the resentment you carry around. Just try to imagine how good you would feel if you weren't always angry or upset about someone or something. I have had to do this myself. I start by imagining it, and then after a while of doing that, releasing the anger and disappointment becomes more manageable.

Recently I attended an event called "Oprah's Lifeclass" in NYC, hosted by Oprah Winfrey and Deepak Chopra. During the event, Oprah and Deepak spoke a lot about karma, clarifying that although different cultures have different names for it—including the Golden Rule or even Newton's third law of motion—it all essentially means the same thing. As Newton explained, for every action there is an equal and opposite reaction. The Golden Rule says, "Do unto others as you would have others do unto you"— sort of like what goes around, comes around. Karma is basically destiny or fate, as determined by your previous actions.

One thing I took away from this class was that we do not have to worry about what we've done in the past. Even if we've messed up and done bad things, that doesn't mean we're doomed and our lives are ruined. Deepak said that karma is the ultimate free will; your life is determined by every thought and every action you have in each moment. He also said that when you do better in each moment, you compensate for past moments when you behaved poorly. You can erase your karma by being better now, for the now is all you have.

A wonderful prayer says, "The past is gone, the future is not here, and now I am free of both." What you do at this moment determines how you live in the future. Dana didn't sit across from me and say that she hated the man who had raped her and thrown her off of a cliff. Nor did she say, "Karma is a bitch; he'll get his." She demonstrated unbelievable compassion for this man, understanding that each of us is a product of our individual circumstances.

As blogger and poet Melanie Moushigian Koulouris writes, "Once you become consciously aware of just how powerful your thoughts are, you will realize that everything in your life is exactly how *you* allow it to be." This could not be more important to remember than when you're choosing how to work with resentment.

Freedom comes in forgiveness and letting go. When you free yourself of your past resentments, you release yourself of the worry of the future. Soon, magically, your life will become exactly what you want it to be.

WAYNE'S RESPONSE

I have often told my children that before I incarnated into this lifetime I had a conversation with God, in which I told Him/Her that all I wanted to do for this entire journey was to be a teacher of self-reliance, and God responded by saying, "If that is your true intention, then we better get you into an orphanage for a decade or so, where you will come to know self-reliance firsthand, and then no one will ever be able to dissuade you that such a thing is not always possible."

As Serena mentions in this chapter, she's often heard me tell the story of how I was directed to my father's grave when I was 34 years old. I was filled with rage and resentment over the fact that this man not only abandoned me, but my mother and two brothers as well. For a large part of my life that resentment resided deep within me, and I had a ready target for dispensing my blame. It was all my father's fault that I was so unhappy and angry . . . all of this wasted, gloomy energy directed toward a man I had never even met. He walked out when I was an infant, and my resentment, which I of course justified, was keeping me from fulfilling a destiny that was always just outside of my grasp.

At his grave site on August 30, 1974, I was practically ordered to practice forgiveness by my source of being, who was reminding me of my prenatal intention to live and teach self-reliance. In one Divine moment I was able to send love, where hatred and bitterness had previously resided, to my biological father. And everything in my life changed. My writing shifted, I focused on living from a place of health, I gave up alcohol, I began an exercise regimen that was to last for the rest of my life, success and happiness began to chase me, my love relationship was transformed—all because of a profound moment in which I discarded blame and replaced it with forgiveness.

The significance of removing blame and practicing forgiveness cannot be overstated. Serena writes from her heart in this chapter about her relationship to her older sister who has struggled with a prescription-drug addiction. As she has heard me say frequently, "Who am I to judge another of God's children and to blame them for my state of mind? People do what they know how to do, given the circumstances of their life." This is what I did at my father's grave, and this is what Serena is practicing with her sister.

A single act of forgiveness turned my entire life around. It has been my intention to not only live a lifetime of self-reliance, but to teach this idea to all of my children as well. On a daily, and sometimes hourly, basis, I would remind them that the only way they will ever be truly free is by accepting total responsibility for how they feel about everything that shows up in their lives. I would remind them incessantly that no one can make them unhappy unless they consented to such a state.

Blaming others for one's misery means that you have to wait for the person you blamed to change before you can experience happiness. And that, of course, is a fool's paradise. This is the opposite of self-reliance.

When my children would say to me that I, as their parent, should fix things so that they could be happy, I'd respond, often to their chagrin, "Parents are not for leaning upon; they are to make leaning unnecessary." After saying these things for their entire lives, the message slowly began to sink in. There is no room for any resentment toward anyone; it is simply an excuse for not taking charge of the reins of one's life. I love this line from Elizabeth Gilbert: "As smoking is to the lungs, so is resentment to the soul; even one puff of it is bad for you."

The story that Serena related in this chapter about Dana, who was raped and thrown off of a cliff to die, is illustrative of all that is implied in this chapter on no justified resentments. When I first met Dana several years ago, she was just as trapped in her mind as she was in that wheelchair. She was filled with rage and revenge, unable to control her colon, and she looked like a sad, defeated soul. Today she is able to walk with some assistance, she has full control of her bowels, and she looks simply radiant. She practiced what St. Francis beseeches us to do in his famous prayer, "Where there is hatred, let me bring love." By replacing her hatred with love, Dana has become a spiritual alchemist. Serena has developed a binding friendship with Dana, and as a result of that comradeship, my daughter has learned firsthand the significance of eschewing all resentment and becoming her own student of self-reliance—and from a student, she has emerged into a teacher as well.

Many years ago, I saw a column in the newspaper that said, "Resentment is letting someone you despise live rent-free inside your head." This is the problem with justifying any and all resentments. It takes away your inner peace and turns the controls of your inner world over to others, and often those others are people you dislike and want to stay as far removed from as possible.

Today Serena knows better than to blame anyone else for what she is experiencing within, and this comes after a lifetime of being reminded that she, and only she, is responsible for how she feels. Thousands of times I've shared this quote from James Allen in *As a Man Thinketh* with her, her siblings, and my audiences around the world: "Circumstance does not make the man, it reveals him to himself."

CHAPTER 8

TREAT YOURSELF AS IF YOU ALREADY ARE WHAT YOU'D LIKE TO BE

*"Health, wealth, beauty, and genius are not created; they
are only manifested by the arrangement of your mind—
that is, by your concept of yourself, and your concept of
yourself is all that you accept and consent to as true."*

— NEVILLE GODDARD

When I was a kid and would tell my dad that I didn't think I could do or accomplish something, he'd remind me of Thomas Troward's wise words: "The law of floatation was not discovered by contemplating the sinking of things." Just think for a second how weird your life would be if you had a father who said something like that! That statement, which I heard too many times to count, is both insane and logical at the same time. What we think about expands, Dad would remind me, and I wasn't going to get anything done by sitting around and contemplating my failure in advance. Just because something hadn't been done before didn't mean it was impossible.

I've constantly been reminded that my imagination is my greatest gift, and that I can use it to come up with anything I would like to be or anything I would like to create. After all, everything that exists in the world today was once only imagined. The computer I'm writing this book on was once only an idea in

Steve Jobs's mind. The chair I'm sitting in did not exist until someone came up with the idea of inventing a comfortable chair on wheels. The Starbucks coffee I'm drinking right now exists because Howard Schultz thought that America should have coffee bars like Italy has—and he set out to create them.

Stories like these exist because someone had a desire to create something. They didn't tell themselves, "That's impossible," or "That won't work," or "If that was a good idea, someone would have done it already." Truly successful people find success because they picture themselves having it. They imagine themselves living the life they want to create, and then they go out and create it. As Pablo Picasso said, "Everything you can imagine is real." So if you want to create the life you dream of, you have to imagine it first.

A few years ago my parents introduced me to the teachings of Saint Germain and *The "I AM" Discourses,* which are based on the idea that the name of God is "I AM." The discourses teach that God is in you and all around you, so whenever you say "I AM," followed by something that you want, you call it into being. The converse is true as well: When you say "I AM," followed by something that you *don't* want, you call that into being as well. I have been using these powerful two words as something of a mantra ever since learning about them. In this way, I'm treating myself as *already being love* and *already being peace.*

When we treat ourselves as if we currently are what we'd like to be, we live with the expectation that everything we want is indeed on its way. This isn't about deceiving or lying to ourselves; on the contrary, it is about choosing to believe that the life we want for ourselves is not only a possibility, but is already happening. That is how we make our dreams a reality.

The Feeling of the Wish Fulfilled

Neville Goddard was a brilliant teacher who lived in the 1900s and wrote many books, one of which is called *The Power of Awareness.* Dad sent me this book a few years ago and said that it was the type of book you could read a hundred times, and each time discover something you didn't understand before.

Throughout the book, the author encourages us to "assume the feeling of the wish fulfilled." In other words, whatever it is that we want in life—whatever our wishes are—can be brought into being by assuming the feeling of it already coming true. Neville said that the only way to manifest what we want is to feel it as if it were already there, and then live from that place— in other words, to live from the end. As my dad has said so many times before, "*Feeling* any state you wish to achieve is the experience that impresses it on the subconscious."

As I read *The Power of Awareness,* I would call Dad to talk about it, and we would go over the ideas together. At the same time I kept hearing about these vision boards that people were making. As I mentioned earlier, a vision board displays images of what you'd like to be or how you would prefer your life to look, acting as a visual tool to help you clarify and focus on specific goals. I decided to make one since I have never been good at writing down my goals and adhering to them!

I found magazine photos representing everything I wanted to attract in my life and put them on the vision board. I placed my board in front of my bathroom sink so that whenever I was brushing my teeth, washing my face, or getting ready to go somewhere, I would be able to visualize all the things I wanted to show up in my life. And before I went to bed, I'd think about what it would be like if what I was envisioning actually started to happen. I would fall asleep with these feelings in my system.

At that point in my life, I'd just gotten out of a bad relationship, so I wanted to be in a good one, with the right person. More than that, however, I wanted to have a personal feeling of success and accomplishment. I wanted to have my own career and feel good about myself and what I was doing with my life each day. I had no idea what kind of career I wanted, but rather than despair over that fact, I just concentrated on the *feeling* I would have if I were doing something I felt proud of. I assumed the feeling of the wish fulfilled—the wish was feeling good about what I was doing with my life, despite the fact that I didn't have a concrete idea what that was. I would assume the feeling of being happy with what I had done with myself that particular day, rather than stay in the feelings of shame and guilt I had over not knowing what I was doing with my life. As Carl Jung said, "Your vision will become clear only when you look into your heart. Who looks outside, dreams. Who looks inside, awakens."

Slowly, I began to feel better about myself. I also did start to see some of the things on my vision board show up in my life. But contemplating myself in a happy and peaceful relationship remained a challenge. Specifically, it was difficult not to spend my time thinking negatively about what I'd just gone through. I felt fearful of having another bad relationship, and I had a hard time picturing myself in a good relationship at all. I told my dad about this, and he said that if I'm always thinking negatively about having a partner, then I'm not creating a space for the *right* partner to show up in a new and good way. He told me that if I continued to hold on to a belief system that was negative, I'd just continue to attract more of that same type of relationship.

During this time I was on the phone with one of my friends who was driving to the mall. "Of course it's raining out and there are no parking spots," she said. "Just my luck."

Something about hearing her say this really struck me, so I replied, "No, don't say that! Only say 'just my luck' when really *good* things happen to you! Don't confirm to the universe that you expect bad luck. Affirm that you expect good luck!"

Ever since that moment, I say "just my luck" every time something good happens. I had one friend tell me that I obviously had no idea what the phrase meant because I was using it wrong. I just looked at her and said that I had it right, and everyone else was using it wrong. She thought I was crazy, but I thought *she* was the crazy one!

I have many memories of Dad stopping as we were walking because he'd spotted a coin on the ground. As he bent down to pick it up, he'd say, "Dear God, thank you for this symbol of abundance that continues to show up in my life every day." I thought he was completely nuts and wasting his time . . . until he let each of us have one of the pretzel barrels filled with coins that he had collected over the years from doing just that. My barrel alone had over $400 in it! Then I thought he was a *genius*—and I started doing it, too!

It's interesting that whenever Dad picked up a coin, he made sure to mention that this "symbol of abundance" *continues* to show up, implying that more was already on the way. He didn't say, "Thank you, God, for this one-time deal" or "I am grateful for this one penny and don't expect any more." Instead, he acted as if more was already coming—and it always was!

Anything Is Possible

I became better and better over time at staying aligned with the type of life I wanted for myself. I also became more effective at manifesting into my life the things that I intended to have or the type of person I intended to become. Eventually every single thing I put on my vision board came true. *Every single thing.* I don't think this happened because I am "deserving" or "special." I think things turned out this way because I believed them into reality. I slowly began to treat myself as if these things were already happening, and then they simply appeared.

For example, I put a picture of Oprah and me on my board, and a short while later I had lunch at her house. A few months after that, I wrote an article about my vision-board experience, and Ms. Winfrey herself put it on her website. I was so shocked and grateful. It reconfirmed for me what Neville Goddard had written—that I had the power to fulfill my wishes!

I think one reason my vision board worked so well is that from an early age I have been taught about living from the end and treating myself as if I already am what I want to be, and because of this, I rarely doubt whether or not it will work. I can remember being in elementary and middle school and having to take national standardized tests. These were tests that you couldn't study or prepare for, and since my parents knew this, they encouraged us to remain peaceful and calm as we took them.

During the week of the tests, Mom would tell my siblings and me that we had the knowledge of the whole universe within us. If we relaxed while taking the tests and trusted that we'd do fine, she said, we really would. My parents did not put any pressure on us to achieve at these tests, and we barely discussed them at home. The morning of the tests, however, Mom would hand each of us a Snickers bar. She'd tell us to eat it on break, and let it remind us that we were infinitely wise. She said it would help us stay in the calmness of that understanding.

As I've already mentioned, Mom is the calmest person you could ever meet, so when she said this to us, I felt the strength of her belief. In all of my academic years, even through college, I'd bring a Snickers with me during exams. While everyone else was freaking out during the breaks, I'd be cool as a cucumber.

It also helped that in our household, learning was meant to be fun. We were never told anything negative while studying. No one ever said, "Why don't you understand this?" or "We already went over this; I can't believe you don't remember." If we struggled with a particular subject, we were supported rather than put down.

As a kid, I was forever imagining myself to be smart and successful. I daydreamed all the time, usually that I was doing something incredibly fun like being a chef or a pilot. My babysitter, Kelly, who was like another parent to me, recently told me that I was the most confident kid she had ever met in her whole life. She told me that even if I was genuinely awful at something (like dancing), no one could have convinced me of that—in fact, my confidence actually convinced others that I was great at it! I think this is because in my imagination, I was always doing so wonderfully well. That's how I began to view myself.

In my teen years, and later on when I entered my 20s, a lot of this faded. (Which is probably a good thing, because I may have really hurt myself or someone else if I would've tried out for the basketball team or dance squad!) But I still believe that anything truly is possible for me.

For example, not long ago Matt and I were in Newport, Rhode Island. We went for a walk along the cliffs where all of the enormous mansions are built, and I was lost in some daydream—picturing myself with a bunch of kids running around on the lawn of one of the houses overlooking the ocean, having parties and barbecues with all of my friends and family. Nearby I heard a woman say to her husband, "Can you imagine living here?" Without missing a beat, he said, "No, I can't." The woman said, "I can't, either." I felt like these people were just handing me material to put in my book!

I was never taught to believe that things were impossible; in fact, I was taught the exact opposite. Here I was, picturing my unborn children frolicking around on the lawn of a palatial home. I was absolutely able to imagine myself living there, with no hesitation at all. Meanwhile, I overheard other people announce that this level of abundance was outside the realm of possibility for them.

I told Matt about this big epiphany I was having on the beach, and he told me that when he was a kid, he'd constantly picture himself living a life that was more grand than the one he had. Matt is from Michigan, and he said that he used to walk to school in the snow and imagine what it would be like to live in a tropical place—how much better it would be to walk to school in that kind of environment. As he entered his teen years, he'd envision himself as a successful businessman, able to buy whatever he wanted and driving a fancy car. Even before he was old enough to drive, he imagined himself with a car, driving all over town and seeing new things every day. The day he became old enough to drive, he bought a moped with some money he'd been saving and took off to see three new places in town that day.

My husband is someone who uses his imagination to picture himself in the life he wants—and then he goes out and accomplishes it. Even though he came from a middle-class family in Michigan, he believed that having a lot of success and living in Florida was within his reach. He believed that when he finished high school, it would all unfold naturally for him. He definitely struggled at times and made mistakes, but in the end, he remained steadfast in his belief that he would have a grand future. Sure enough, he does.

Believe It, and You Will See It

A couple of years ago, Dad and I were on a cruise ship in the South Pacific, when a woman approached us with tears in her eyes and said that he had literally saved her life. Her name was Sharon, and she was born and raised in Iran. When the Shah was overthrown and the Ayatollah took over in 1979, she was forced to wear a veil. She wasn't allowed to go to school anymore, and thousands of people around her were executed just for being educated. She went on to marry a terribly abusive man.

Sharon said that she found one of my dad's books that had been translated into Farsi: *You'll See It When You Believe It.* She told us that it was the first time she had ever known anyone to say that in order to see something happen, you have to believe in it first. She said that everyone she knew always said, "Yeah, I'll believe it when I see it." But while reading Dad's book, she realized that her life didn't have to stay the way it was.

Sharon began to believe that she could escape Iran and her abusive husband, even though she had no idea how. Everyone in her family, including her mother, told her to accept the beatings and be a more obedient wife, but Sharon could not do this. She started to see herself in a different life—a life of freedom, where she was actually happy. She said she planted in her imagination the life she wanted to create. Day and night, she would find herself off in a daydream about how wonderful her life would be.

Some months later, Sharon and her family decided it was necessary to leave Iran after she had been jailed for showing a piece of hair through her veil, and they were granted visas to go to Canada. Sharon had more freedom in Canada, but the abuse from her husband continued. After he broke her nose, she knew that it was time to get out of this situation. As frightened as she was, she had to make this choice for herself and her children, so she left her husband and has been free ever since.

Sharon had never before heard the types of things that Dad had written in his books, but somehow she'd put the idea of freedom—from both Iran and her abusive husband—into her consciousness and made it her reality. I feel that even before she discovered my dad, though, she must have been aligning herself, even in a subconscious way, with a better life. She must have been the type of woman who doesn't just accept bad things happening to her, because she had a belief, somewhere deep inside, that she was worth more.

Sharon told us that she'd been praying to meet Wayne Dyer and share her story with him, and now here she was on a cruise ship with him! Well, he was so moved by her story that he asked her if she'd be willing to join him onstage during one of his lectures to share her story with the entire audience. When you align yourself with the power of intention, you never know how much abundance you just might get!

What's so crazy is that Dad's books were banned in Iran at the time Sharon was living there. In the 1970s, another woman named Mariam contacted him and asked if she could translate his books into Farsi. Shortly after that, Sharon got a hold of one of the books, realized that she could believe something into reality, did it, and 30 years later ended up on the same ship with him sharing her story with a large audience. All of this was possible because Dad, Mariam, and Sharon believed it into being.

For me, the real icing on the cake of this story was getting to meet Mariam and spending three days with her in Turkey recently. She'd found out that Dad would be on a trip with a large group of people throughout the Mediterranean, and she came to the port where the cruise ship docked while we were in Istanbul. I was standing with my dad, mere seconds away from boarding a bus to take us to see the various sites, when a woman walked up to him with a sign that said YOU'LL SEE IT WHEN YOU BELIEVE IT. When she asked him if he knew who she was, he said that he wasn't sure and asked her name. She said, "Mariam from Iran"—and Dad started to cry!

I'd heard about Mariam before, and she had sent us things from Iran when we were children, but I couldn't believe that she was actually standing in front of us. She ended up spending three days with us and joined my dad onstage in Ephesus, Turkey, to talk about Rumi, the great Persian poet whose poetry she and Dad had shared through letters for years. Mariam held a vision of being able to meet my dad, and seeing her up there onstage with him, talking about Rumi, made me sob and shake for the entire duration of the lecture they gave together.

I felt a great deal of love for this woman who had believed in my father's work so much that she'd risked her life in getting it published and traveling to meet him. It wasn't even that she happened to love my dad that made me so emotional. What really got me was seeing someone go after what they wanted, even if it took *years* to happen, and witnessing the gratitude she felt for being able to be there.

Meeting Sharon and hearing her story, and then meeting Mariam just a few months later—and understanding that they were all now forever connected to both my dad and myself—was truly a life-changing experience.

So when I hear people say that big things aren't possible, that miracles don't happen, or that the odds are against them, I say, "Never let the odds keep you from doing what you know in your heart you were meant to do."

I have learned that there is a part of all of us that is outside the world of the physical—something that is infinite, even as our body is finite. When something is infinite, it has neither beginning nor end. This inner part of us, our soul, doesn't want "stuff" or "things," it wants *space*. Dad says that the soul needs to be free to expand; to reach out and to embrace the infinite. The soul is not happy when it is restricted because all it wants to do is grow. Anything that comes into your life and attempts to restrict you or hold you back will make your soul miserable.

Being one of eight children, I can tell you that no one wants to be told what to do. No one wants to be slapped around and owned and controlled—we all just want to be left alone to listen to our souls and be who we are. When we're able to be ourselves, our soul grows and expands. This allows us to live out our dharma. When someone tries to restrict us or tell us who to be, what to believe in, who to be like, or what rules to follow, they're doing more than controlling us; they're crushing a part of our soul.

In schools across the United States, there is a trend where children are committing suicide because they feel as if their true nature is being squashed and criticized and attacked. These precious beings are dying because they don't yet know or believe that they can be who they really are.

These children are taking their own lives because their souls are miserable. They're being told that who they incarnated to be in this lifetime is not acceptable, is not right, and is not of God. I wish I could tell every single child that who they are is a spark of God. That they must only love themselves, treasure their own magnificence, and know that they can create for themselves the life that they want.

Learning to accept some of the bumps in the road in my own life has helped me get to a place where I can adhere to the vision I have for myself, without allowing anyone else to take me down. When there is turmoil in my life, I am able to imagine peace, to understand and know that I will eventually go back to feeling peace, and that the turmoil is temporary. This has helped me be able to continue to treat myself as if the life I want is already happening, even at the times when it seems that it isn't.

We should all be inspired by people like Sharon and steadfastly believe in the life we want for ourselves, no matter what the odds are. Place your dreams into your imagination, and just watch what happens.

The Gift of Real Magic

On that same cruise where I met Sharon, I also met Ann Steward. She pulled me aside and said that she had a story she wanted to share with Dad and me. Her story touched me so much that I wanted to include it in my book, so I asked her to write it down for me. Here it is, in her own words:

I traveled to Fiji a little over a year ago for a combined conference and holiday. After meeting local villagers on the Coral Coast and attending their church, what should have been a soulful Sunday turned into a human tragedy. I was sitting watching the sunset when I saw Juitassa, a man who worked in the hotel I was staying in, light the torches that line the beach every night. Suddenly, he himself caught alight. He had used his right arm to light the torch, when his grass skirt blew in the wind and his whole body caught fire. It was like a scene from a Hollywood movie—dreadful.

I screamed at him to roll in the sand, and made the split-second decision to run back to my room to call emergency, and to get wet towels and water to cover him. It took 85 minutes for the ambulance to arrive. It was awful seeing Juitassa lying in the sand and smelling his skin burning. I kept rushing back to my room to get water to keep his skin cool, and other people came to assist. He was in shock and was slipping in and out of consciousness. I kept talking to him to try to keep him conscious.

Over the next six days that I stayed in Fiji, I visited Juitassa daily in the hospital. He had suffered third-degree burns over half his body. I met his wife and tried to assist where possible. At the same time, I had grave concerns about his welfare, as the standards at the hospital were certainly below what I was used to. What struck me was the strength that Juitassa and his wife showed through all of this. Even though he was heavily sedated, I could see his fighting spirit.

I had to go back to Australia, as I have a family and work responsibilities. I was very concerned about Juitassa, though—I contacted the hospital repeatedly to check on his progress, but was never given any information.

The next month, I found out that Wayne Dyer was speaking on a cruise that would soon be departing from Australia. I have followed Wayne's teachings for years, and his words of wisdom had gotten me through an incredibly difficult time in my life. I knew that I wanted to see him. The thought was intensified when I found out that the cruise ship was stopping in Lautoka, Fiji—which meant I would have an opportunity to check on Juitassa.

The cruise was completely booked, but I didn't let that stop me. I kept manifesting the intention to go. I even contacted the cruise organizers in the USA, and to my delight, there was a cancellation two weeks before the cruise began. I booked my reservation, and we set sail.

The stopover in Fiji was one week into the cruise, and I remember being apprehensive about what I would find when I went to see Juitassa in the hospital. To my delight, he was progressing well. It was hard to believe that it had been only two months since I'd seen him, because his skin was healing remarkably well. After we'd spoken for a while, he asked what I was doing back in Fiji. I explained that I'd had the opportunity to go on a cruise with a remarkable spiritual man whose words of wisdom I followed. But I'd also wanted to go on the cruise because the ship was stopping in Fiji and it meant that I could see him.

Juitassa was interested in the "speaker" and asked me questions about him. I was trying to keep it simple, as Juitassa had a limited education. I said that the speaker was a great spiritual man who taught about the power of the mind and the soul to heal both the body and the heart. Juitassa asked more questions and became quite excited.

He told me that he had the same beliefs—that every day, he and his wife would pray and visualize his body becoming stronger and his skin healing. He said that they would close their eyes and visualize his skin as smooth and completely healthy again. He pulled back the sheet so that I could see his feet, which is where he had started the visualization. Sure enough, his skin had started to heal!

Juitassa asked me the name of the man I had traveled so far to see. I said that they probably had not heard of him in Fiji, but his name was Dr. Wayne Dyer. Both Juitassa and his wife exclaimed with surprise. His wife pulled open the drawer next to the bed, and took out a Wayne Dyer book. It had been left in the waiting room of the hospital shortly after I had left the first time. You can imagine my astonishment.

The book was *Real Magic,* and Juitassa's wife had been reading it to him daily. It was from this book that they had gotten the idea to meditate and visualize. Talk about serendipity! Here I was, traveling on a cruise ship with the intention of seeing Wayne Dyer and at the same time, taking the opportunity to see how Juitassa was healing. Only to find out that somehow, Wayne's insight into the human spirit had reached out to this poor man in a developing country. That somehow, through the power of intention, Juitassa had understood the concepts of meditation and visualization and was using them himself to heal!

Juitassa had even gained the insight that though the accident was tragic, it was meant to be for some reason. He didn't understand the reason, but he knew that one day he would. This is a man who has had few opportunities in life; who only a week before the accident had been granted sponsorship to immigrate to Australia as a tree lopper. This is an opportunity that comes once in a lifetime for someone like Juitassa. Of course, with the third-degree burns and ongoing skin grafts that will be needed, he has lost that opportunity. Still, he remains optimistic and strong.

All I know is that I was meant to be on that cruise, and that somehow Wayne's message had connected between him, Juitassa, and myself, and had become the key to his healing.

When Ann told me this story, I was blown away! I was so amazed that this man's wife was reading to him from one of my dad's books, and that Juitassa—a native man on the island of Fiji—was not only applying the principles he was hearing, but they were working for him as well. Juitassa was using the principles in *Real Magic* to create what he wanted, which was the healing of his burns. He was treating himself as if he already had what he wanted to create: a healthy body. He was open to the idea that he could visualize his burns as already healed, and as a result what he was experiencing was rapid healing.

I am so inspired by this man, and by Ann, too. She happened to be in a certain place at a certain time, witnessing this horrible situation. But because she went out of her way to help and take care of him, her life has been positively affected by this whole situation as well. Ann will tell you that Juitassa has become an inspiration in her life. Had she forgotten about him after she went back to Australia, she wouldn't have experienced this miraculous story either. Both Ann and Juitassa demonstrate for me the idea that when you serve others without asking "what's in it for me," you benefit as well. To that end, when I shared Ann's story with Dad, he promised that he'd send her more books and audio programs for Juitassa to enjoy while he was in recovery in the hospital.

Juitassa, Sharon, Mariam, and so many others have shown me that when you visualize the life you want to create, miracles happen. As I said before, *A Course in Miracles* defines a miracle as *a change in one's perception*. The people I have written about in this chapter have changed their lives because they changed their perception of what their lives should look like or what was possible for them. Viktor Frankl wrote that in order to survive the concentration camps, people had to change what they believed to be true about themselves. And as my dad always says, when you change the way you look at things, the things you look at change.

Let's all be encouraged to use our imagination to visualize the type of life we would like to have, and then align ourselves with that energy. Remember, we do not get what we want; we get what we are. Become what it is you are seeking, offer yourself to the world, and enjoy the results!

WAYNE'S RESPONSE

The greatest gift that any of us are granted is the gift of our imagination. Every single thing that now exists was once imagined, and the corollary of this assertion is that everything that is ever going to exist in the future must first be imagined. In my role as a father and a teacher, I felt it was incumbent upon me to help my children understand and apply the phenomenal implications of this basic notion. "If you want to accomplish anything," I would tell them, "you must first be able to expect it of yourself. If you can't imagine it, you can't create it."

What I have noticed in my life is that most people do not have even an inkling of the power that exists within them if they learn to apply the extraordinary capacity of their own minds. I have had many long conversations with Serena about this very thing. It was the inspiration behind her story of her vision board, as well as her own decision to reprogram herself to believe that when she said "just my luck," she meant her good luck, rather than the opposite idea that most people have adopted. Whenever my children and I would be driving and looking for a parking place, they frequently heard me say, "I have a spot to park—be on the lookout for it." They never once heard me say, "With my luck, we'll never find a place to park."

From being able to produce a parking place to creating a one-on-one meeting with Oprah Winfrey to manifesting a perfect relationship, it all boils down to how one uses this Divine gift of their imagination.

There simply are no limits. As Serena confirms in this chapter, I told my children repeatedly and incessantly that when they place something into their imaginations, and hold on to it as an inner vision as if it were affixed with superglue, that is how they align with their source of being. It is a way of being a co-creator with God, who is responsible for all of creation. This is how they connect with their senior partner, and this is how the whole process of manifestation unfolds.

I have written extensively about this power of manifestation, and my children regularly heard me say, "If you place your thoughts on what you don't want, don't be at all surprised if what you don't want keeps showing up in your life." Similarly, I encouraged them to avoid placing their thoughts on what others expected of them, or on what had always been, or on what was difficult or impossible, unless that was what they wanted to manifest into their lives. It was always my objective to help them be in awe of the amazing capacities of their minds, and the thoughts that they employ on a daily basis. I reminded Serena regularly to not even place her thoughts on "what is" if she didn't like what she observed about what is.

I learned a long time ago from one of my mentors, Dr. Abraham Maslow, that self-actualized people never, but never, place anything into their imaginations that they don't want to harden into an objective fact. They use this great gift of their imagination to keep it always centered on what they intend to have manifest into their lives.

I often told my children a story I made up about a person who was given a million dollars to go out and purchase anything they wanted. When that person went to the mall, they spent their money on everything they didn't like, and asked to have it sent to their house. Then when they arrived home, they asked, "Why is my house filled with so many things that I despise?" And the answer I would shout is, "Because they're crazy! They were given currency to purchase whatever they wanted, and they spent all of their money on what they didn't want." Then I would tell them that their thoughts are their currency for purchasing what they want—so if they kept their thoughts on what they didn't want, or what used to be, or what somebody else wanted for them, then they were crazy, too.

Living as if you already are what you would like to become is really tapping into the spark of God that exists within. In the book of Romans, Saint Paul speaks of God, saying that "He calls those things which do not exist as though they did." This is living from the end, which is the great secret of manifestation. Acting as if that which is placed in the imagination is already an accomplished fact, and never letting go of that inner picture, is what I want all of my children to understand. The use of the two magic words *I am,* which Serena cited in this chapter, is a wonderful technique for aligning with one's source of being. These are the words spoken to Moses when he asked for the name of the spirit that spoke to him in the form of a burning bush that was not being consumed.

The use of these two words to declare what you want to materialize, such as *I am perfect health* or *I am in a Divine relationship*—even if your senses tell you otherwise—is how your highest self operates on this earthly plane. Albert Einstein once made this observation about the power of our imagination: "Logic will take you from A to Z. Imagination will get you everywhere." As a parent, I want my children to get to places where so many refuse to contemplate, and this is why I encouraged all of them to use the greatest gift they've ever been given, and to be in awe at the endless possibilities.

CHAPTER 9

TREASURE YOUR DIVINITY

"You have been criticizing yourself for years and it hasn't worked. Try approving of yourself and see what happens."

— LOUISE HAY

When we were little, my brothers and sisters and I were taught by our parents that God resided within each of us; that our divinity was not something we needed to go out and look for. Instead, we would find it when we looked within.

In our house, there were tons of different religious symbols all around. We had laughing Buddhas and framed words from Christ. We had copies of the Torah, the Tao Te Ching, and the *Bhagavad Gita*. We went to a Christian school, but we were encouraged to question what they taught us—rather than accept it as the truth just because it was being told to us. We were raised with the idea that if we learned about divinity from every perspective, we would ultimately realize that we were Divine ourselves.

From an early age we were taught that we are all pieces of the one creator, whatever you want to call it, and that we all came from there and will return there. We were also taught that all matter, all thoughts, and all beings are energy. The great creator is the energy of all of us, and being a part of it is what makes us all one. We often discussed the idea that everything is energy and that's all there is to it. Match the frequency of the reality you want and you cannot help but get that reality. It can be no other way. This is not philosophy. This is physics.

Treasuring your divinity simply means accepting all parts of yourself as having come from pure, Divine love. I know that there are times when loving yourself and feeling worthy as a human being are really challenging. There are times when we all doubt our self-worth and feel lacking in different areas of our lives. But to treasure your divinity is to *know* in the deepest part of your being that you are worthy of love, that you come from a place of perfect love, and that you *are* love.

When I join Dad on his cruises, he and I often walk the perimeter of the ship and talk about various things that are on our minds. He said that ever since he was in the Navy, being on the ocean reminds him of God. As he's told me many times, we are all pieces of God, every single one of us. We all come from God, but we are also all made up of God. He explained that if you take a cup and fill it up with water from the ocean, what you have in that cup is ocean. You don't have the entire ocean in that cup, nor do you have its cumulative size and strength, but you *do* still have ocean in that cup.

Human beings are little cups of God. We may not be as big or as strong as God, but we are all still God, for that is what we are made of. If I were to take that cup of ocean water and place it on the ship's deck, eventually the water would evaporate and return back to the ocean. But while the water is in a separate container, it loses the power of the entire ocean force. It simply isn't as strong as the rest of the ocean.

This is the secret reason to treasure our divinity. When we feel disconnected from our source, we lose our own Divine power. Of course, just like the cup of water, we will eventually all change form and go back to our source. But we don't have to die to be connected to God. As long as we see ourselves as God, we have access to the power of God—which, as Dad once wrote, "is the unlimited power to create, to be miraculous, and to experience the joy of being alive."

Dad always says that the cup of water, when it's disconnected from its source of the ocean, is the symbol for the ego. I've previously mentioned the ego in this book, but just as a reminder, it is that voice that insists you're the sum total of what you have, what you do, and what other people think of you. Your ego tells you that you're not connected to others, but instead are separate from everyone.

Many of us have an ego that is in constant competition with others. It contends that we live in a world of limited possibilities and finite opportunities, so we must beat out everyone else to make sure we get our share. Basically, our ego tells us that we shouldn't be happy for people who get what they want, because their success hurts our own chances of being happy. Since there is limited abundance, we can't all get everything we want, so we need to compete with our friends and trust no one.

The most challenging aspect of the ego is that it convinces us that we're separate from the things we want, so we must chase them down. When I think about the idea of chasing something that is missing from our lives, I picture a man with a chainsaw running down the street trying to make friends—not understanding why everyone is running in the opposite direction! We can't chase anything; we can only align with it.

The worst part about the ego, in my opinion, is that it convinces us that who we are is limited to our body and our personality; that these two things are separate from God. Our ego tells us that God is outside of us, something to fear and seek approval from, just like all those other egos we're competing with. We suddenly believe that we must ask God for special help in stopping all those other forces from taking what we feel is rightfully ours.

As my dad once wrote, "Your ego keeps you in a constant state of fear, worry, anxiety, and stress. It implores you to be better than everyone around you. It beseeches you to push harder, and to get God on your side. In short, it maintains your separate status from God and allows you to be terrified of your own divinity."

Become What You Seek

When I was little, I was taught that the prayer of St. Francis was not just a prayer; it was a *technology*. By saying, "Lord, make me an instrument of thy peace, where there is hatred let me bring love," you are employing a technology—just like running a program on your computer. You're asking to become a servant of God's love, and the universe will respond.

Technology is not dependent on you, whether or not you've been a good person or have caused harm. If you know how to use a keyboard and a mouse, you can use your computer. If you know the prayer of St. Francis, you can run the program of peace and love in your life. Reciting this prayer, carrying it around with you, contemplating it, or even just reading it will help you understand that it is in giving that you receive. Serving others, and *yourself,* is the greatest act of love on the planet.

By becoming a servant of God's peace, love, and compassion, you're not only helping others receive these things, you're receiving them yourself. We are all connected, all part of the same energy and same universe, so when you serve others, you are serving that highest part of yourself. When you serve others, you are also serving God.

When you live from the knowing that we are all pieces of God, pieces of this great creator and energy body, you will, as Mother Teresa said, see the face of Jesus Christ on the streets in your own neighborhood, every day. You'll begin to realize that we are all Divine, and that when we live from this place, we are tapped into the power of intention and can create the life we want. This isn't like the teachings in the book *The Secret,* which suggests you can want things and they will come. It is much deeper than that. You actually have to *become* what you are seeking, by offering it to others first.

I experienced this intimately a few years ago, when Sands, Saje, and I accompanied our dad on a trip to three of the most spiritual places in Europe. We went with a group of 150 people, all of whom wanted to experience these places with Dad. If I'm honest, I'll admit that I wanted to go because it was free, and I love traveling. I knew it would be fun to go with Dad and my siblings, but I didn't know that much about the point of the trip when I originally signed up to go. So before we left, I did some research on the three places we'd be visiting.

First we were going where St. Francis lived, taught, and was buried in Assisi, Italy. The second location was Lourdes, France, where Saint Bernadette was born and received visitations from the Virgin Mary. After that, Lourdes became the site of many miraculous healings. The vision also prompted Bernadette, then just a young girl, to become a nun—who would eventually be recognized by the Catholic Church as a saint. The final place was Medjugorje, Bosnia-Herzegovina, where several teenagers received visitations from the Blessed Virgin multiple times, and many continue to receive them to this day.

Of course I knew about St. Francis of Assisi, because his prayer hung in the hallway in our home, right outside of the bedroom I shared with my sisters. I hadn't heard much about Medjugorje or Lourdes, though, and I realized that both of these sites were directly related to Blessed Mary. I felt really happy about this, as I'd always wanted to know more about her and have a stronger connection with her. I had gone to a Christian school as a child, but it wasn't a Catholic one, so we didn't learn very much about the Virgin Mary. I knew that she was the mother of Jesus, but I didn't know much else. As a woman, however, I had always felt drawn to her and Mary Magdalene.

As I researched the trip, I became the most excited about visiting Lourdes and learning about St. Bernadette. I was especially intrigued after I learned that she had an "uncorrupt body." I had to Google that term, and couldn't believe what I discovered: St. Bernadette's body had not physically deteriorated since her death in the 1800s. Better yet, she was displayed in a glass coffin, so you could actually go to the church and see for yourself!

From the time we arrived in Lourdes, I found myself in a perpetual state of prayer and gratitude. Those were probably the most peaceful few days of my life. We had just left Assisi, and

Lord, make me an instrument of thy peace was running through my mind like a mantra. I felt like I was in a constant state of prayer, always asking how I might serve, not concerned with what was in it for me. I was really contemplating the idea of being an instrument of God's grace in my everyday life, and I was passionately praying to be used to do more good in the world. I had also just finished reading a book on St. Bernadette and was grateful to be where she had lived.

In the evenings in Lourdes, thousands of people from different parts of the world and different religious backgrounds would gather together and walk in a parade, with everyone singing "Ave Maria" and chanting prayers out loud. Those who were sick or injured were pushed in wheelchairs in the front of the parade, and everyone else followed behind, praying for them and everyone else in the world. It was a really amazing and miraculous thing to take part in. I was brought to tears multiple times throughout my visit to this remarkable place.

While we were there, I received an e-mail from a family friend named Gary Liebl. Gary had recently come back from Lourdes and had seen on my Facebook page that I was there. He wanted to tell me that one of the highlights of his life was being dipped in the holy waters of the grotto, where it is believed the Blessed Mary instructed young Bernadette to dig. The water that flows from this spring is known to have healing properties, and there is now a building erected over it. Men and women wait in separate lines to enter the building, one by one. Accompanied by nuns or monks, depending on your gender, each person removes all of his or her clothes and is dipped into the holy waters. This process is called "the healing of the sick by the immersion in holy water." Gary was writing to say that I should really try to do this if possible, because it was so impactful on him and his spirituality. I read his message and although it sounded neat, I thought that taking my clothes off in front of some nuns was probably not my thing. I decided to keep an open mind, however, in case the opportunity came up.

Lo and behold, later that same day a woman on the trip asked Saje and me if we had experienced the healing of the sick by the immersion in the holy water. We said that we had not. She told us that it had been truly amazing for her, and if we had the chance, we ought to try it. This was the second time someone went out of their way to bring this up to me. In my mind I said, *Okay, if this is meant to be, give me one more hint. Then I will do it.*

The next day, Sands, Saje, and I were in the lobby of our hotel, getting ready to do a tour of the home Bernadette lived in as a child. A woman and her daughter, who were part of our tour group, came rushing up to us and said that they'd just got back from the immersion in the holy water. They said we *had* to do it. I looked at Sands and Saje and told them we were doing it. I'd gotten three signs, and you just don't ignore this kind of thing.

At first Sands told us he was not "getting naked with a bunch of old dudes." But when I told him that our friend Gary from Maui had done it, he reluctantly agreed. We told the woman that we would go over to the springs after the tour. She said that we had to be in line by 2:30 P.M. to make it into the baths before they closed. I looked at my watch and it was 2:10! It was our last day in Lourdes, so we had to go then. We ran across town to where the line was supposed to be and waited for ten minutes before we realized that we were in the wrong place. When we found the actual location, Sands was able to walk right in to the men's line, but Saje and I were told that the women's line was already closed. They said the wait time was over two hours, and they had to close by 5 P.M. We were too late.

Saje and I stood at the gate and decided to wait there for our brother to come out. A woman from our tour group who was already in line came over to us from inside the gate and asked if we had done this yet. We told her we hadn't, and we weren't going to make it. She said she had already done it, and she wanted to give us her spot so we could experience it. She told one of the security guards to let us in so we could have her spot, but the guard said he couldn't open the gate. He said only the main man in charge could open it again, and he pointed us in that man's direction.

The woman from our group approached the manager from inside the gate while we waited outside. She told him that we *had* to get in—we were young and had come all the way from America, and this was our only chance. The man had at least 15 other women begging from outside the gate to get in, and he quietly shook his head at everyone. He said that he just couldn't make the nuns stay any longer, and we should all come back tomorrow. The woman from our group wouldn't give in that easily, though. She kept pestering him, pointing at Saje and me, showing him how young we were. (For some reason she thought this really mattered!) Finally he looked over at us. When he met my eyes, he stopped.

"You want that woman to get in, that one right there?" he asked, while pointing directly at me. The woman from our group said, "Yes! Her and her sister."

"I will let her in because I know what she did," he said. I felt all the color drain from my face. I thought, *Oh no, he knows what a sinner I am. He sees that I need this more than anyone. I must have done something really bad.*

The man motioned for Saje and me to come to the gate, and he had security hold the other women back so that my sister and I could walk in. I was trembling when I approached him. "I saw what you did with that elderly woman today," he told me. "You can go in, and you can cut the line. You don't even have to wait, go right ahead." I looked at him and I began to sob. I knew what he was talking about. Everything hit me all at once.

Earlier in the day, Sands, Saje, and I had been walking to get lunch when I saw an elderly woman sitting by herself in a café across the street. As I watched her, she dropped her walker. I waited to see if someone was going to help her. When no one did, I walked across the street, picked up the walker, put my hand on her arm, and said, "God bless you."

She smiled and thanked me, and I went on my way. I didn't even think of it as any big deal. I had been praying for God to make me an instrument of love and peace, and stopping to help this woman just seemed like the right thing to do. It turns out that the man in charge of deciding who could cut the line was sitting in the same café and saw the whole thing happen.

As I entered the area where you remove your clothes and dip into the holy water, I couldn't stop crying. I was overcome with the feeling that when we come from a place of kindness and service, without expecting a result, we receive from God ten times what we give. I had actually lived it briefly that day. I was so grateful to have become an instrument of God's grace, even just for a moment, as I had been praying to be.

Before the nuns dipped me in the water, they told me to "set my intention" and then recite with them a Hail Mary and the Lord's Prayer. I set my intention to always be an instrument of God, because the feeling of it was beyond anything I could have anticipated.

I left the baths rejoicing, crying, laughing; I was ecstatic. I probably looked like a lunatic on the street, but I didn't care. I felt great.

What I discovered that day is that we all have the option to live a life filled with miracles—where we receive everything we want in the world and more. The way to live that life, I realized, is to become what it is we want, and to offer it to others.

One of the most important things I learned from this process is that you can't offer love toward others without offering it toward yourself as well. You must understand that you yourself are a Divine creation, worthy of love. When you feel this toward yourself, you are able to give it more freely to others. You must become love in order to give or receive love.

I am not a very holy person. I don't sit on my knees and ask for forgiveness all day and chant prayers. I seldom attend church. I live my life in a very normal way. I call my siblings names (we use "Idiot" and "Nasty" as terms of endearment), and I like to poke fun at myself, my friends, and my family members. I do all of these things from a space of love, but still, I do them. I curse in traffic and sometimes get road rage. I lose my temper easily and sometimes drink too much and start fights with my husband. I still battle to not engage in mean gossip. I am a completely normal person who lives in a completely normal way.

The only thing I do that is really different is ask to be a being of love in my everyday life, to lift up those around me without asking for anything else in return. We don't have to go anywhere or be anyone special to come from a space of love. We only have to try, in each moment, to do a little better and help a little bit more. And if my experience is any measure, we ourselves benefit as much or more than those we are helping.

Turning Negativity into Love

When I felt stress and fear as a child, Dad would tell me to go get a pitcher and fill it with my fear. "I can't fill a pitcher with fear," I'd say. "It's just something in my head!"

"Exactly," he would reply. "There is no fear. There are just people thinking fearful thoughts."

As *A Course in Miracles* says, if you knew who walks beside you on this path you have chosen, you would never experience fear or doubt again. I can really feel the beauty of those words. They remind me that I don't need fearful thoughts; I am choosing to have them, so I can choose to have thoughts of love instead. There are only two emotions in the world, fear and love. That which is fear cannot be love, and that which is love cannot be fear. If you notice that you're having fearful thoughts, replace them with thoughts of love. Pray to become an instrument of love toward everyone, and practice catching yourself when you are engaging in thoughts of harm toward others. When you do, simply stop yourself and say, "I am love I am." Over time, you will have fewer and fewer of these thoughts. Instead, you will live in a beautiful space of peace and joy.

If we're struggling with turning hatred or fear or anger or sadness into love, then we must change our concept of ourselves. What I mean is that we must change what we believe to be true about ourselves. To become human beings who are open to changing—who know that we are capable of changing. If we continue to believe that we're not capable of changing, then we're going to stay exactly where we are. If, however, we're willing to try something new, believe something different, and have a mind that is open to everything, we will be able to embrace our divinity and know that anything is possible.

There are many things in our world we cannot change. One thing we *can* change is how we live our lives in response to our surroundings. We can start by catching ourselves whenever we have a thought of harm, criticism, or condemnation toward anyone, including ourselves. We can then change our behavior, making our new way of being into a habit.

This shift does not come from a place of superiority. If I think I'm going to be nice to my neighbor who acts like a jerk because I am superior to him, I'm barking up the wrong tree. Instead, I'm going to be nice to everyone and everything because nice is all I am inside. Recognizing that I *am* divinity, I realize the Divine is all I have to give away. I believe this is what St. Francis was saying when he asked to be made into an instrument of thy peace. He wasn't saying, "Dear God, I have no peace. Please give me a little of it." What he was saying was, "Let me *be* peace. Let me be peace so that the only thing I can do is convert hatred into love, turmoil into tranquility." When you become like what you desire, you align with it and it comes to you.

Those who treasure their own divinity, who follow what is inside of them, who follow their own inner calling and pay no attention to the good opinion of others—I call these "self-actualizing people." Self-actualizing people have a vision, a burning passion, and they follow *that*. They are in tune with their own divinity, so they don't have to pay attention to what other people are doing. They don't have to follow the herd, as Dad always says. They simply follow their own inner compass.

When we catch ourselves having negative thoughts and actions and turn them into positive ones, we begin to move toward a place of Divine love. It's Divine love that will change the world—not war, not violence, not hate, only love. The only place we can begin to experience Divine love is within ourselves. When we are in a state of love toward ourselves, we're able to follow our inner callings and our inner passions. What other people think or feel about us ceases to matter. And what other people are doing in their own lives ceases to matter to us, either. We get to a space where we leave the judging to someone else. We simply exist in a space that is peaceful and supportive of us as individuals.

As I've already mentioned, our parents didn't like it if my siblings and I talked negatively about anyone. Yet I have been around families who make fun of others for the way they are—often right in front of their kids. It baffles me! Demonstrate that it's acceptable to bash and ridicule people, and you're giving your kids the tools they need to become a bully. As the saying goes, "Our children are watching us live—and what we are shouts louder than anything we can say."

If we want our children to treasure their own divinity, we must model it for them. That means we don't put other people down; but it also means we don't put *ourselves* down, or weaken ourselves for the benefit of others. As Marianne Williamson put it in one of my favorite quotes of all time:

> Our deepest fear is not that we are inadequate. Our deepest fear is that we are powerful beyond measure. It is our light, not our darkness, that most frightens us. We ask ourselves, Who am I to be brilliant, gorgeous, talented, fabulous? Actually, who are you not to be? You are a child of God. Your playing small does not serve the world. There is nothing enlightened about shrinking so that other people won't feel insecure around you. We are all meant to shine, as children do. We were born to make manifest the glory of God that is within us. It's not just in some of us; it's in everyone. And as we let our own light shine, we unconsciously give other people permission to do the same.

As we are liberated from our own fear, our presence automatically liberates others.

Whenever I spend time with my mom in a public place, I notice how she takes the time to be kind to everyone she meets. Same for my dad—when we go to a restaurant, he always asks the server where they're from or otherwise engages in conversation with them. If I go somewhere with either of my parents, the staff tends to vie for the chance to serve us. It happens because my mom and dad are simply kind to them, making them feel special.

I am trying to be more like my parents, but it's not so easy for me. Sometimes I still find myself having negative thoughts. Rather than condemn myself, however, I try to replace those thoughts with a little offering of love.

Clearly, I am at the beginning stages of changing my negative thoughts to thoughts of love. But I have to say, I notice shifts already. My habits *are* changing, and I find that I can even give positive thoughts to people who piss me off. (Sometimes, at least.) The change really started when I realized that being angry or negative only poisons my own divinity and peace. Why on earth would I do that to myself? Just to be right or feel justified? Today, even when I know I'm right and I have a justified reason for being angry or upset, some part of me can't go to negativity as quickly. There's a voice inside that says, "Who cares? What is the point of holding on to those feelings? Is this your highest self you're answering to and serving, or is this your ego?"

These two sides are often battling it out inside of me. First, there is the side that loves to argue. It speaks fast, becomes almost blind to my surroundings, and spews abrasive thoughts and words. In my mind, this voice feels justified. It tells me I'm right; my anger and resentment are a proper response to what's been "done" to me.

At the same time, there is another side of myself that patiently observes it all. This is my divinity; my highest self. Even amidst the storm, this part of me remains peaceful, calm, and loving.

It patiently waits for me to finish my rant so that at the end of it, when my ego is satiated, I can return to a place of calm and peace. When I do finally calm down, I usually experience the sour taste of regret. I see that all along, amid the anger and sadness and resentment, I was rejecting my highest self—who only wanted peace. It wants so much to be a source of this Divine peace for others. During my egofest, however, I contributed to the violence that exists in the world. I perpetuated the exact energy I want to get away from.

Dad tells me to catch and correct myself when I'm having thoughts of harm or negativity toward others. I think what he's telling me is to become a person who embraces her own divinity —not just to talk about love, not just to tell other people to live in love, but to actually do it myself. To elevate the consciousness of the world by being a person of God. To me, being a person of God doesn't mean having no fun. It doesn't mean no partying, no zest for life. What it does mean, however, is that I become a person who is fun and exciting to be around because others feel safe and loved in my presence—to become a person who loves them as God does. This is who I am striving to be, and I get closer to it every day.

I'm learning to change the way I process all that happens around me so that I don't set out to create more experiences that cause these feelings. I'm working on not condemning myself when I mess up, and not harboring guilt or shame when I do something dumb or bad. Instead, I try to observe the negative feelings I sometimes feel toward myself until I am able to let them go. My relationship with myself is getting really strong as a result, and my relationships with others are getting better, too.

I've started filling my life with people who serve my highest self. Those who do not, I release in a very peaceful and loving way (most often without letting them know I'm distancing myself from them). The truth is, I am thankful for all of the difficult people who show up in my life. They help me remember who I do not want to be.

Then there are those people who teach me who I *do* want to be. At the top of that list is my best friend, Lauren. I am truly blessed to have her in my life—so much so that it is hard for me to put it into words. Although I'm louder and more gregarious, she has always been the teacher, and me the student. Lauren has experienced unimaginable loss in her life, but through it all, she has remained a beautiful person. She has never given up or given in, and she's never felt pity for herself. Instead, she offers the wisdom she gained to others who are also experiencing great loss. Lauren has learned how to align herself with serving others, and she lives in joy as a result. Learning to turn her own suffering and loss into love and acceptance means that she carries a far greater sense of peace than most other people I know.

As Jesus once said, "Even the least among you can do all that I have done, and even greater things." Again, each of us is a piece of God, a Divine creation that showed up at the exact moment we were supposed to. We will leave at the exact moment we are supposed to as well. In the meantime, we are charged with being the love we came from. For each of us is part of the eternal perfection, which has no accidents. We are all creations of Divine love—we only have to learn to treasure the divinity that exists within each of us.

WAYNE'S RESPONSE

It was always my objective to have my children believe in the central idea of this chapter, that indeed they were all Divine creations and should always treasure the fact that they carried God around with them wherever they went. I would frequently remind Serena and her siblings of the words of Jesus, "It's the spirit that brings life, the flesh counts for nothing." I would tell them that they emanated from the spirit, and that the spirit is nothing more than pure love. The flesh—that is, their bodies—is not who they truly are. Who they really are is a piece of what they came from, and that is Divine love.

Throughout the Bible there are numerous references to the idea that we are all children of the most high; we are all Gods. I often showed my children these passages so that they would remain in deep appreciation for the fact that they carried around a spark of God with them wherever they might go. Serena used the metaphor of a container of ocean water, which must be just like what it came from, and the ocean is a representation of God. Similarly, I would explain that a rock is hewn from a mountain and therefore has the same nature as the mountain, but when it is disconnected, it is no longer called mountain, it is called rock. Its essence remains the same as the mountain, yet pulling it from the mountain has made it something else. Put the rock back in the mountain, and it is no longer a rock. Therefore, the rock's existence is determined not by its substance, but by its relationship to the mountain, which is its source. And so it is with us—our existence is determined not by our fleshy substance, but by our relationship to our source of being, which is Divine love.

"Divine love," I would tell Serena, "is very different from human love. It is the love that our source has for us. It never changes and it never varies. You came from this Divine love, which is so very different from human love, which is always changing and varying in degrees. Treasuring your divinity means always loving and respecting yourself."

If my sons or daughters ever engaged in any kind of self-deprecating talk, I would remind them that when they put themselves down, they were being judgmental toward the very wisdom that created them; in essence, criticizing God for His handiwork. As long as the rock stays connected to the mountain, it literally becomes the mountain.

Serena had a great deal of difficulty in accepting the idea that she actually carries God around with her wherever she goes, and therefore she is God and that is what looks out from behind her eyeballs. I showed her John 10:34, which states emphatically: "Is it not written in your law, 'I said, "You are gods"'?" And Psalms 82:6 from the Old Testament clearly states, "I said, 'You *are* Gods, and all of you *are* children of the Most High.'" I told her over and over to respect her Divine nature, which means to abandon her false self, the ego, and practice being like God. That is, become a being of sharing rather than focusing exclusively on her own self-interest.

This idea of her seeing herself as God was contradictory to so much of what she was learning in her religion classes at school. She was being told to fear God—in fact, those words instructing her to fear God were actually imprinted on a report card she brought home. I repeatedly told her that fear and God could never co-exist because God is love, and why would anyone want to be afraid of love? I made a phone call to the school that she attended and asked the principal to remove those printed words from their report cards. I reminded this Christian-school administrator that Christ stated specifically that God is love, and that all of God's creations are in fact instruments of love. Therefore, fear did not belong in the same context as God.

Serena's story of what transpired in Lourdes—when she was granted entrance to the holy-water baths as a result of her acting from her highest self—is an example of how this teaching was impacting her in her daily life. I'd long encouraged her to persistently stay in a mode of service to others. I recall how excited she was on that day when the gatekeeper allowed her to come to the head of the line because he had observed her reaching out to an elderly woman who needed assistance.

"It's a miracle!" she kept shouting at me. "I thought we weren't going to be admitted to the baths, and all because I acted out of love, my wish was fulfilled. It's really a miracle, Dad!" I'm trying to convey her enthusiasm and excitement here, but words could never describe how thrilled she was to be able to experience firsthand the holy water of Lourdes.

We are saturated in a world where so many people have come to believe that God is an external being, an old white man with a long beard who watches over everyone and dispenses favors to those who fear and obey his written words. And so many of those words are so antithetical to a God of love. My children were exposed to these ideas on a daily basis, and I didn't want them to live with such insane ideas. I wanted them all to know that they came from a place of well-being and Divine love—and this is how I see God, and Jesus as well. I've often quoted these words of Gandhi in my lectures and in my communications with the children: "I like your Christ; I do not like your Christians. Your Christians are so unlike your Christ."

It was my intention that all of my children learn to live from the perspective that the great poet Hafiz speaks about in this, one of my favorite poems that Serena has heard me recite onstage, and directly to her many times as she was growing up (my thanks to Daniel Ladinsky for the translation):

> Even
> After
> All this time,
> The Sun never says to the Earth,
>
> "You owe me,"
>
> Look what happens
> With a love like that,
> It lights the whole Sky.

This means to become a being of love, to know that God is not a distant presence; rather, it resides within all of its creations. Our number one priority is to learn to become like God and to suspend the nagging promptings of the ego, which is nothing more than a false idea of who we really are. This is our highest calling, and this is what Serena was speaking about in all of her poignant examples in this chapter.

CHAPTER 10

WISDOM IS AVOIDING ALL THOUGHTS THAT WEAKEN YOU

"You don't have a soul. You are a soul. You have a body."

— ANONYMOUS

As I've said many times in this book, thoughts are energy. The vibration of our thoughts are as real as the vibration of light, sound, heat, magnetism, and electricity. This isn't just spirituality; it's science. So if we accept that our thoughts are energy, then it stands to reason that wisdom could be defined as avoiding thoughts that weaken us. There is a connection between our thoughts and their impact on our bodies. Medical researchers have proven long ago that a stressful thought can create an ulcer. If you go to a doctor and you have an ulcer, the first thing they're going to ask you is what kind of stress you have. Our thoughts definitely impact our bodies.

When I was about 15 or 16, I came home from school with a couple of my girlfriends. Dad was in the kitchen reading a book called *Power vs. Force,* by David Hawkins, M.D., Ph.D. He said that he'd just discovered the ultimate lie-detector test and wanted to show me how it worked, right then and there. Since I was not the type of kid to be embarrassed by my parents, and since my friends typically thought my family's weirdness was cool, I agreed.

Dad told me to hold my right arm out and think about something that I loved. Facing me, he used two fingers to push down on my arm. My arm remained strong, and I was able to resist his push. Then he instructed me to think of something I didn't like, and to hold my arm up just as I had done before. This time when he pushed my arm down with two fingers, it went completely weak.

My friends didn't believe what they were seeing. They thought I must have just let it go weak to prove Dad's point.

"Okay," he said. "Let's do it again. This time, tell me something that I might not know is a lie or not."

"Natalie is dating Jack," I replied. This statement was not true, and sure enough, my arm went weak. Dad explained that lies weaken you, while the truth strengthens you. So we kept at it, working through a bunch of lies and truths with my friends. The muscle testing worked every single time.

My sister Skye—who was always a goody-goody—had come home during this time and wanted to try out what we were doing as well. While Dad was asking her questions and showing her that lies weaken her, my other sister Sommer told him to ask Skye if she had ever smoked pot. Sure enough, Skye's arm stayed strong. Then Skye told Dad to ask Sommer that same question. I swear I have never seen Sommer move so fast out of a room in my life!

Dad was really excited about this book and the possibility of muscle testing. *Power vs. Force* offers a way of understanding and actually mapping how thoughts either strengthen or weaken you. The book explains that power allows you to live and operate at your best without effort. Force, on the other hand, requires movement. Power is an energy field that does not move, but rather stands as it is. Force, on the other hand, creates motion. Motion creates counterforce, which uses energy.

Dad helped clarify the difference between power and force by giving the example of an athlete at a sporting event. If the athlete's entire focus is on beating their opponent and winning at any cost—on force, in other words—then the muscular structure of their body will be weakened. If, however, their thoughts are focused on performing at their highest capacity and using their own inner strength to excel, they'll actually *strengthen* their body. There is no counterforce to consume their energy, so they'll be empowered. It was clear that power thoughts strengthen us, while those of force weaken us. If thoughts of love strengthen our arm muscles and negative thoughts weaken them, imagine what our thoughts do to the rest of the muscles in our bodies—especially our hearts!

According to Dr. Hawkins, the thoughts that weaken us the most are those of shame. Shame is inwardly directed, based in a hatred or dislike of ourselves or our actions. Shame not only weakens us physically, but emotionally as well. For this reason, loving and forgiving ourselves is incredibly important. The easiest way to let go of thoughts of shame is to let go of the past and to live in the now.

The other emotions Hawkins says negatively impact us include anger, guilt, and apathy. I was taught that anger, like resentment, happens when things don't turn out as we want or expect them to. Anger and resentment can seem like normal thoughts to have, but they greatly weaken us. They often spur thoughts of revenge and violence, which are forces that create counterforces. As the proverb says, "Before you embark on a journey of revenge, dig two graves."

Then there's guilt. My dad often says that no amount of guilt will undo what has already been done. We do not learn from our mistakes by staying stuck in the guilt of them—we learn by allowing our mistakes to move us forward, by not choosing the same behavior that made us feel guilty in the first place. We release thoughts of guilt by choosing empowering thoughts of love and respect for ourselves. Dad maintains that the true test of nobility is to vow to be better than we used to be. It isn't about beating ourselves up for our mistakes; it's about making a commitment to do better in the future.

Apathetic thoughts are those that keep us from being fully engaged in life. Being apathetic is like being uninterested in everything around you; uninterested in life, basically. In my house, *bored* was a bad word. Mom and Dad would tell us kids that boredom was the same as apathy. They insisted that having nothing to entertain us or fill our time was a great opportunity for us to use our imagination to create something for us to do.

One Saturday morning when we were little, we were sitting on the couch watching TV while Mom made breakfast. I mistakenly yelled out, "I'm bored!" Our mother came into the living room and told us all to get up and go outside, and then she actually locked us out! At first we were all surprised, and then I got yelled at by my siblings for what I'd done. About two minutes later, we were in the pool and had forgotten all about breakfast and our boredom.

To this day, when I hear kids tell their parents they're bored and the parents jump to entertain them or switch the channel on the TV, I cringe. I never thought I would make *bored* the bad word in my own house, but I definitely see that happening now!

Mom always asked us, "How can you be bored when you have an imagination and can go outside?" Our babysitter, Kelly, was the same way. Kelly wouldn't allow us to play video games or watch TV when she was with us—instead, we used our imaginations. A favorite pastime was to make and direct our own movies. She would film us making the movie, the commercials, and even the credits. We have literally hundreds of home movies and commercials made during the time we might otherwise have been watching TV.

Kelly also liked to drive my siblings and me out west in Florida to the horse farms. We would pick up bags of apples and carrots on the way and spend an afternoon feeding and petting the horses, rather than hanging out at the mall. My sisters Sommer and Saje eventually became so enamored with visiting the horses that they signed up for lessons. Over time, they both became champion horseback riders.

All of our lives, my brothers and sisters and I were taught that the antidote for boredom and apathy is awe. When we choose to view our lives and the world around us as awe-inspiring, apathy can't really exist. Whenever we'd roll out of bed in a bad mood, Dad would tell us that we had the choice each day to say, "Good morning, God!" or "Good God—morning!" Whichever we chose would determine the outcome of our day. If we chose to see each day as a beautiful gift filled with endless opportunities for exploration and discovery, then that's just what we would find. If we chose to view each day as just another battle to fight, then that is what we would find as well.

As the title of this chapter reminds us, wisdom is avoiding all thoughts that weaken us. So in order to cultivate wisdom, we must learn to focus our energy on the positive, which strengthens us both inside and out.

Thoughts of Strength

When we believe we aren't good enough, not worthy of love or acceptance—when we condemn ourselves and wish we were someone else—we weaken our physical bodies. My friend Anita Moorjani, author of the book *Dying to Be Me,* learned this first-hand. After years of living a fearful life and feeling inferior, she became so ravaged by cancer that she was ready to give up. Yet she had a near-death experience that turned everything around for her. She did not die; in fact, she found out how to truly live. She was taught so many profound lessons during this experience, including this one:

> In truth, I'm not my body, my race, religion, or other beliefs, and neither is anyone else. The real self is infinite and much more powerful—a complete and whole entity that isn't broken or damaged in any way. The infinite me already contains all the resources that I need to navigate through life, because I am One with Universal energy. In fact, I *am* Universal energy.

Getting to know Anita and reading and rereading this quote has given me new insights into the way my best friend, Lauren, decided that she wasn't going to live in fear. Even after her mother passed away from cancer, Lauren felt that obsessing over whether or not she would also be stricken by the disease would only make her more likely to get sick. Lauren knew that we get what we think about, whether we like it or not. So she decided she wasn't going to think about getting cancer—she wasn't even going to entertain the idea that it was an option for her.

She didn't believe that she was any more likely to get the disease than anyone else; instead, she believed that cancer was passed down from one generation to the next through the way women model their mothers' and grandmothers' ways of handling their emotions and their relationships with themselves. Lauren saw how her mother always held everything in, sacrificed herself, and willingly accepted suffering as a necessary part of her life—and she felt that had resulted in cancer. In other words, the cancer came from the way Lauren's mother processed her emotions and her life events, rather than from her genes.

Not long ago, Lauren called me from London to tell me that she was in so much pain she couldn't move her body without screaming. This lasted for a few days until she finally went to the hospital to get herself checked out. After a series of tests and doctors' visits, Lauren was told that her blood work indicated that she had some sort of an autoimmune issue. Her doctor said that because her levels of inflammation were so high on three different blood tests, she needed to take steroids and a bunch of other medications as well.

Lauren and I began researching what something like this could mean, and we were both pretty heartbroken by what we found. She came to stay with me for six weeks, and we talked about it every day. Ultimately, Lauren decided that she wasn't going to accept any diagnosis. She felt that what she was experiencing was temporary, so she was going to treat it that way. She stopped taking all of her medication because the side effects were really dangerous and damaging to other organs in her body. Instead, she decided to start meditating on the question of why she had gotten sick in the first place.

At the end of her visit, Lauren told me that she felt she'd received this diagnosis because she felt judgmental toward her mom for being sick all those years. She said that sometimes she hadn't had as much compassion toward her mother as it had seemed.

I know how dedicated and compassionate she was toward her mom, so I believe that my best friend was experiencing guilt over a time or two when she lost patience, and was wallowing in that feeling.

Anyway, Lauren said she was going through this because she had something to learn about illness, but she was confident she wouldn't have it for the rest of her life. She was beginning to have a greater sense of love and compassion toward her mom, who had been sick for so many years. She said she realized that she'd been holding on to guilt and shame over the times she had lost her patience with her mom while she was sick, and that she was in the process of forgiving herself for that as well.

Shortly after Lauren got back to London, she went to the clinic to meet with her doctor, mostly to see how her levels were doing now that she hadn't been on any medication for several weeks. To her surprise, her regular doctor and two of his colleagues came into the room to tell her what they were seeing. As God is my witness, the doctors told her that all of her levels had gone back to normal. It was something they had never seen before. The chief physician at the clinic said that in all of his years of treating patients, he had never seen someone's inflammation levels return to normal—especially not someone who had stopped all medication.

Lauren called me from the clinic ecstatic, and I cried and cried on the phone, purely overjoyed! She then e-mailed me copies of her recent blood tests, as she had done with her previous tests, so that I could see with my own eyes her new, normal blood levels.

Many of us, especially women, are taught that we're not worthy of love—that we shouldn't expect miracles and that great things just don't happen for us. There's a current belief that suffering is a normal and expected part of life, and that sacrificing oneself over and over again is a great way to become a hero. I wasn't taught this way. I was raised with the idea that I should always think thoughts that made me feel good; that I should expect miracles; and that I was not just *worthy* of greatness—greatness was already on its way! Lauren's experience just confirmed that expectation.

As Viktor Frankl writes in *Man's Search for Meaning*:

> For what then matters is to bear witness to the uniquely human potential at its best, which is to transform a personal tragedy into a triumph, to turn one's predicament into a human achievement. When we are no longer able to change a situation —just think of an incurable disease as inoperable cancer—we are challenged to change ourselves. . . . But let me make it perfectly clear that in no way is suffering *necessary* to find meaning. I only insist that meaning is possible even in spite of suffering— provided, certainly, that the suffering is unavoidable. If it *were* avoidable, however, the meaningful thing to do would be to re- move its cause, be it psychological, biological, or political. To suffer unnecessarily is masochistic rather than heroic.

To suffer unnecessarily, or to readily take on suffering so that others don't have to feel it, is to harm yourself. Suffering doesn't actually help anyone else. That said, if you're in a situation where you cannot avoid suffering—like Dr. Frankl, who was in Auschwitz, among other concentration camps—you must change your way of thinking. And changing your way of thinking means changing yourself.

⌒

A few years back, my dad was diagnosed with chronic lympho- cytic leukemia—a form of leukemia that is not treatable, but is also not life-threatening as long as it doesn't shift into an acute form. He received this diagnosis at a time in his life when I, as his daughter, knew he wasn't completely at peace. He was regularly on edge, often in a state of turmoil. He was in a relationship that I would describe as toxic, but he was completely enthralled by it. When he received the CLL diagnosis, it seemed clear to me that his body was responding to how he felt in that relationship.

Since then, many people have asked Dad why, if he believes that illness stems from emotions, did he get sick? I would say to these people that my father is a human being, a regular man just like anyone else. Although he is a great teacher and has lived his life on a spiritual path, he's still human. Being spiritual is like having a full-time job; you have to work at it. At least, that is my opinion.

I realize this may sound radical, but I try to remain open to everything—especially new ways of thinking about illness and healing. When Dad began to change the way he viewed his leukemia, the leukemia itself began to change. His healthy numbers began to rise, and his leukemia-indicating numbers began to decline. Today, he lives in a state of belief that he is leukemia-free and is no longer doing testing for it. Everyone tells him that he has never looked healthier, and he feels amazing as well.

Some people may argue that giving up testing is careless or he's just avoiding his illness, but I believe that we all leave our bodies and this planet when we're supposed to. The way we choose to spend each day is what really counts, and Dad made the decision not to spend any more of his days sitting in waiting rooms contemplating being sick. He actually views the leukemia as his body's way of coping with certain emotional stresses and said that he feels grateful for it. He has no issue with it, whether it is still present or not.

I love having parents who see things this way. I can't remember a time in the last ten years that my mom went to the doctor for something other than a broken bone or injury. She gets acupuncture, and that is the only form of medicine she is completely comfortable with. I like knowing that we can look at our lives in different ways, and that whatever we choose is just right. Perhaps the way we choose to look at things actually changes the outcome. You may agree, you may disagree, or you may feel neutral about it. Whichever is true for you, you are right.

When you choose thoughts that remind you of how beautiful you are, how perfect you are, and that you are a piece of God, you actually strengthen your physical body. If you can change the way you think, you can change the way you live. This is just as Mom and Dad raised us—to have a mind that is open to everything and attached to nothing. As John Maxwell wrote, "You will never change your life until you change something you do daily."

Living from Love

In the words of the poet E. E. Cummings, "To be nobody-but-yourself—in a world which is doing its best, night and day, to make you everybody else—means to fight the hardest battle which any human being can fight; and never stop fighting."

Dad used to say this to me as a child all the time, and I'm so glad he did. For all of my weirdness, quirkiness, and uniqueness, I wouldn't want to be anyone else. Oprah told all of us at the Lifeclass I attended that we are not our body. We are a soul, and we are using a body. To look at someone else and judge them on the basis of the body they incarnated into in this lifetime—or to judge *yourself* for the same thing—is to miss the soul! You are a soul, and so am I; infinite, deathless beings that operate only from a place of pure, Divine love. When we allow ourselves to believe that we *are* our bodies, we allow the ego to take over. This isn't something to battle—it's just something to observe.

At that same Lifeclass, Deepak Chopra explained that when the ego makes us feel small, we usually experience a tightness somewhere in our bodies. Our negative thoughts actually manifest in our bodies in a physical form. For example, sometimes I feel bad because I still feel judgmental toward people in my life. It's like there's a contest being waged between my ego and my higher self. Even though I want to improve myself, to align with my highest nature, I am still feeding my ego. That battle is the ultimate melodrama! But Deepak reminded us that there is no point in battling our egos; we can only observe them. When we experience tightness in our bodies, we must simply observe it until it goes away.

I experience tightness in my chest whenever I know I did something wrong and am afraid of getting caught. What I have learned through meditation is that if I observe my emotions along with the tightness, I avoid feeding them. Eventually, they go away. I don't have to confess my sins, or ask anyone outside of myself for forgiveness. I only have to forgive myself and love the parts of me that still do bad things from time to time.

What I'm pointing toward is that we have to become like God; to live from God's love. If we can direct this love toward others, and especially ourselves, our lives will be filled with miracles. Deepak urged us to notice when we start to have thoughts about being better than or separate from others—not to engage in the chatter, but to simply observe it. For example, when I'm alone at night I often feel scared. Sometimes I get so scared in the dark that I have an inner dialogue to calm myself down. I'll say to myself, "Calm down, Serena. You are fine." But then another part of my mind will reply, "No, you are *not* fine! You should be scared and on edge. If you aren't, then something really bad could happen." This goes on and on until I eventually fall asleep. While I used to engage in the dialogue, now I just observe it and breathe into the feelings of fear. Knowing this, I sleep much better!

The truth is, there are a lot of people I know, myself included, who feel like worrying is *necessary*. We feel like the constant mind chatter is a really important part of our lives. What we don't realize is that it takes us out of the present moment. When we become absorbed in worry, we miss so much of the beauty that is around us. Not only does the worrying cut us off from those around us, it cuts us off from the world. It fuels the feeling of separateness from everything and everyone. "The stronger the feeling of separateness," Eckhart Tolle says, "the more you are bound to the manifested, to the world of separate forms. The more you are bound to the world of form, the harder and more impenetrable your form identity becomes."

When we engage in thoughts that separate us from others, from the world, and from God, it becomes harder and harder for us to tap into the power of intention. This is the life force that allows all things to become manifest, that allows us to create the life we want. So we must choose our thoughts carefully. I was always encouraged to move away from feeling angry, resentful, fearful, and guilty to a place of strength. I was encouraged to choose thoughts that remind me that we are perfect creations of God, worthy of love for that reason alone.

I am blessed to have parents who taught me to live in this way—who taught me the ten secrets in this book and raised me to understand that I was the master of my fate and the creator of my destiny. Growing up, I learned to be open-minded, to follow what I was most passionate about, and to focus on loving myself first, so that I could offer love to those around me. My mother so beautifully modeled for me the benefit of embracing silence, and my father taught me to give up my personal history so I could experience all the glory of living in the present. I learned that in order to change a problem in my life, I had to change the way I was thinking. I learned one of the biggest lessons of life— that there are no justified resentments. I learned the art of manifestation and thinking *from* the end, rather than *about* the end. From my parents and so many of the influential teachers in my life, I have learned to treasure my own magnificence, and that I am very much a piece of God's perfection. Finally, I have learned that we become what we think about, like it or not, so we might as well choose thoughts of love, forgiveness, and strength.

For all of this, I have my parents to thank. As my dad once said to my mom: "I thank you like the earth thanks the sun. Everything I am is because of your unconditional love. Thank you, thank you, thank you."

WAYNE'S RESPONSE

I have long been intrigued by the power of our thoughts. The mind-body connection is a fascinating area of inquiry, particularly in the field of applied kinesiology. On many, many occasions I have brought people up onstage to demonstrate how muscle testing can reveal which of our thoughts are serving to strengthen us, and which are making our muscles go weak.

I would ask a volunteer to deliberately tell me a lie, such as to falsely say that her name was Mary Jones and then swear to it; as I muscle tested her, the lie would always make her arm go weak. Then she would give me her real name, and much to her astonishment, the same arm would remain firm and I would be unable to push it down. I then began to have volunteers think of a moment when they felt shame, and without revealing the details, simply stay in the feeling of being ashamed. Without fail, in one hundred percent of the times I used this demonstration before thousands of people, every thought of a negative emotion—such as shame, fear, worry, sadness, or rage—revealed the same reaction when I pushed down on their arm. They would always go weak simply because of the thoughts they were selecting at the moment.

Our body's basic health is impacted on a continuing basis by how we choose to utilize this amazing human attribute called our mind. On one occasion, my son Sands was listening to some loud music with violent and profane language blaring out over the speakers in the house. I asked him to remove the CD and bring it to me. I then did a muscle test by having him first hold an organic apple over his heart, and I was unable to even budge his strong extended arm. Then I had him replace the apple with the CD containing the offensive language, and he immediately went weak. He was in shock.

Serena's examples from our many family evenings of fun and enlightenment over how our thoughts impact every muscle in our bodies was a part of my effort to have all of my children learn to change, on the spot, any thoughts that might have a deleterious effect on their bodies. "Your heart," I would tell them, "is one huge muscle, and it is seriously impacted by any thoughts that are unhealthy for your own well-being."

When they would ask me how a thought that was a lie could possible make their muscles go weak, I would remind them that their bodies all came from a source of perfect love, which is Divine truth. When they would abandon that truth, which is their very source of being, by telling a lie, they would put their bodies into a weakened posture, a place that is foreign to their very creative essence. I frequently quoted the poet John Keats's observation that beauty is truly the expression of God's wisdom: "Beauty is truth, truth beauty,—that is all / Ye know on earth, and all ye need to know." When you leave truth, I would tell them, you are literally forsaking your source, and this will always weaken you.

For most of my life I have been an advocate of the power of the mind to heal, while still maintaining a healthy respect for the medical community. I wanted all of my children to be mindful of their own innate capacities to ward off disease. I would tell them that they all had a pharmacy within their own system that could create whatever drug they needed—such was the nature of their own biological perfection. I witnessed Serena's best friend, Lauren, heal herself by adamantly refusing to accept the dire prognosis she'd been given. I have applied this kind of "weird" thinking to my own body throughout my life, and I continue in this modality today.

I know that my every thought has an impact on all of the organs in my body. Every day I stay in a state of gratitude for the *I am* presence that is always with me. I call upon it whenever any discomfort or signs of impending illness begin to surface. I know that my thoughts will either assist me in staying in a place of well-being, or enhance the ability of the disease to immobilize me. Having all of my children be fully aware of this innate power to heal and manufacture any needed medicine, without having to obtain a written prescription, was something I wanted them to see firsthand.

On the exit door to my writing space at my office I placed a simple written observation, which I read every day. It said, ATTITUDE IS EVERYTHING, SO PICK A GOOD ONE. This was my daily reminder to be cognizant of my thoughts, and to persistently remember that any and all negative or fearful thoughts could and would impact everything I experienced each day—most especially, my own physical health. When we would do the kinesiology experiments at home, which were always fun and filled with reactions of shock and disbelief on the part of the children, it was basically done to have them understand that their attitude toward everything had an impact on this bewilderingly perfect creation called their own bodies.

All I wanted for my sons and daughters, and for all of those who read my books and attended my lectures, was to realize that they could always choose a thought that would empower them, as opposed to ones that make them fragile and weak. Indeed, the title of this final chapter summarizes one of the greatest lessons we can all use each and every day of our lives: wisdom is avoiding all thoughts which weaken you. Or as the children heard me say so many times, "Your life is a product of all of the choices that you have made, so choose well."

ACKNOWLEDGMENTS

I would like to take a moment to thank every person in my life who has supported and encouraged me throughout this process. I began writing this book in 2010, and it took me almost four years to complete it. I don't know if I would have been able to finish it had it not been for the constant love and inspiration of my friends and family. Special thanks to:

My parents, first and foremost, for their belief in me and constant friendship. Dad, you have taught me how to stand on my own two feet. I hope this book serves as a reflection of your lifelong work of being my teacher and my parent. I am so grateful I "picked you," and I love you so much. Mom, you are the angel in all of our lives, the wind beneath all of our wings, and our biggest fan. I love you so much.

The entire Hay House team, especially Reid Tracy, for his patience and understanding while I navigated my way through writing my first book. And to both of the women who edited and shaped my book, allowing it to be as it was meant to be, while simultaneously making it a thousand times better!

My siblings, Tracy, Shane, Stephanie, Skye, Sommer, Sands, and Saje, who have always been the greatest friends I have ever had. Tracy, I admire your humor, intellect, and wit, not to mention your great bag line! Shane, my older brother, I love your gentleness, your strong moral sense, and your kind heart. Stephanie, you are strong, smart, generous, and so hard working, and I love you. Skye, I admired you my whole life growing up—you light up every room you enter and show grace in all aspects of life. Sommer, you are the funniest and most intelligent person I have ever had the privilege of knowing; thanks for always loving me. Sands, you are the most precious man I have ever known. You are so kind and beautiful inside and out, and I believe in everything you stand for. Last but not least, my little sister, Saje. I have loved you to pieces since the moment you were born. You are wise, pure, and honest.

My sister-in-law, Julie; and brothers-in-law Mihran (Mo) and John, who have only added to the joy and love I feel in our family. I am so grateful to my eight nieces and nephews who have reminded me how to live in the moment, how to be in awe of the world we live in and find the joy in every experience, no matter how small. Carter, Tysen, Thatcher, Devyn, Fischer, Parker, Grayden, and Westyn—you are the greatest nieces and nephews in the world, and I love you all enormously!

My friends, who provide me with endless laughter, funny stories, wine nights, and bonds that have lasted for more than 14 years and counting. Ashley and Natalie, my lifelong gayles, problem-solvers, and beautiful friends, I am so grateful for your constant friendships in my life. My childhood babysitter, Kelly, thank you for shaping so much of my childhood with your gentleness and reverence for all of life. Lauren, you are my best friend, soul-sister, and closest confidante, and the most honest and trustworthy person I have ever known.

My stepson, Mason, who in his young 15 years has taught me so many things about myself, particularly how rewarding it is to love and raise a child.

Finally, my love, Matt. Your patience, dedication, and love for me bring tears to my eyes. You are the man I love.

— **Serena**

ABOUT THE AUTHORS

Serena J. Dyer is the sixth of Wayne and Marcelene Dyer's eight children. Serena attended the University of Miami, where she received bachelor's and master's degrees, and now lives in South Florida with her husband. She spends her time traveling, reading, blogging, cooking, and working to combat child trafficking through several local organizations.

Dr. Wayne W. Dyer is an internationally renowned author and speaker in the field of self-development. He's the author of more than 40 books, has created many audio programs and videos, and has appeared on thousands of television and radio shows. His books *Manifest Your Destiny, Wisdom of the Ages, There's a Spiritual Solution to Every Problem,* and *The New York Times* bestsellers *10 Secrets for Success and Inner Peace, The Power of Intention, Inspiration, Change Your Thoughts—Change Your Life, Excuses Begone!, Wishes Fulfilled,* and *I Can See Clearly Now* have all been featured as National Public Television specials.

Wayne holds a doctorate in educational counseling from Wayne State University and was an associate professor at St. John's University in New York.

Website: www.DrWayneDyer.com

⤫

We hope you enjoyed this Hay House book. If you'd like
to receive our online catalog featuring additional information
on Hay House books and products, or if you'd like to find out more
about the Hay Foundation, please contact:

Hay House, Inc., P.O. Box 5100, Carlsbad, CA 92018-5100
(760) 431-7695 or (800) 654-5126
(760) 431-6948 (fax) or (800) 650-5115 (fax)
www.hayhouse.com® • www.hayfoundation.org

Published and distributed in Australia by: Hay House Australia Pty. Ltd.,
18/36 Ralph St., Alexandria NSW 2015 • *Phone:* 612-9669-4299
Fax: 612-9669-4144 • www.hayhouse.com.au

Published and distributed in the United Kingdom by: Hay House UK, Ltd.,
Astley House, 33 Notting Hill Gate, London W11 3JQ • *Phone:* 44-20-3675-2450
Fax: 44-20-3675-2451 • www.hayhouse.co.uk

Published and distributed in the Republic of South Africa by: Hay House SA
(Pty), Ltd., P.O. Box 990, Witkoppen 2068 • *Phone/Fax:* 27-11-467-8904
www.hayhouse.co.za

Published in India by: Hay House Publishers India, Muskaan Complex,
Plot No. 3, B-2, Vasant Kunj, New Delhi 110 070 • *Phone:* 91-11-4176-1620
Fax: 91-11-4176-1630 • www.hayhouse.co.in

Distributed in Canada by: Raincoast Books, 2440 Viking Way, Richmond, B.C.
V6V 1N2 • *Phone:* 1-800-663-5714 • *Fax:* 1-800-565-3770 • www.raincoast.com

Take Your Soul on a Vacation

Visit www.HealYourLife.com® to regroup, recharge, and
reconnect with your own magnificence. Featuring blogs, mind-body-spirit
news, and life-changing wisdom from Louise Hay and friends.

Visit www.HealYourLife.com today!